The Lived Horizon
Of My Being

Special Studies No. 29

The Lived Horizon Of My Being

The Substantiation of the Self & the Discourse of Resistance in Rigoberta Menchú, MM Bakhtin and Víctor Montejo

JUDITH THORN

ASU Center for Latin American Studies Press

ARIZONA STATE UNIVERSITY

Tempe

The ultimate dialog is to put into being
an utterance which is both
inside and outside of time.

MICHAEL HOLQUIST

The trouble with life is that it is so daily.

RITA C. CHASE

Published by ASU Center for Latin American Studies
Arizona State University
Center for Latin American Studies
Box 872401
Tempe, AZ 85287-2401

Published in the United States of America.

Cover art by Cliff Gerrish, Pace Design Group, San Francisco
Editing, book design and typesetting by Evelyn Smith de Gálvez.
Proofreading by Irma V. Guzmán

Library of Congress Cataloging-in-Publication Data

Thorn, Judith.
    The lived horizon of my being : the substantiation of the Self & the discourse of resistance in Rigoberta Menchú, MM Bakhtin and Victor Montejo / Judith Thorn.
        144 p.   cm. -- (Special studies : no. 29).
    Includes bibliographical references (p. 129-134).
    ISBN 0-87918-084-6
    1. Self (Philosophy)--History--20th century. 2. Menchú, Rigoberta. 3. Bakhtin, M.M. (Mikhail Mikhailovich), 1895-1975. 4. Montejo, Víctor, 1952- . I. Title. II. Series: Special study (Arizona State University. Center for Latin American Studies) ; no. 29.
BD450.T554 1996
199'.7281'089974--dc20   96-28276
                                                                              CIP

Contents

Foreword

Ethics and Self-Empowerment in Rigoberta Menchú and Judith Thorn

Since the mid-1980s, an extensive body of work has gradually accumulated in academic circles about the testimonial nature of the text that renders the life of Mayan human rights activist and 1992 Nobel Peace Prize recipient Rigoberta Menchú (b. Uspantan, 1959). Surprising as this might seem, very few of them actually deal with the limit-experience of the life behind the text, but are more concerned with the nature of the textuality as such.

The *Popol-Vuh*, sacred text of the Maya-Quiché peoples of present-day Guatemala, written by anonymous authors in the 1540s,[1] tells us how human beings were created from a mix of yellow and white corn. Corn, the center of belief, is a sign of group identity. This explains the sacred character of agriculture. Corn is what gives meaning to ethnic identity and to a cultural universe. Corn has a "mythic" value, not a commercial one. *Corn* is an emblem for the Mayan community. Individual kernels are of no consequence as such.

In similar fashion, Menchú does not see herself as an individual in the traditional modern Western sense. She is an emblem, an icon of her community. She, too, is *corn*, rather than an individualized kernel without mythic value. This apparently simple explanation helps explain the sense that Rigoberta Menchú has of telling not her personal story, but the story of her people. The meanings of the Quiché people are no longer assigned by the order of heaven. They must be achieved. This means that their social group must in turn be made semiotic—receive the mark of meaning.

When the revolutionary process of 1978-1982 destroyed the traditional system,[2] a new aesthetics of identity becomes necessary. An active semiotic process in which the Quiché people are newly emblematized with significance follows the previous system of assigned meanings. In that context, Rigoberta Menchú pictures herself as a shamanistic storyteller. She names things and gives order to their meaning. She explains the nature of Quiché costumes and beliefs—in short, a different view of the world—to engender, with numbing humility, a new centrality for the Quiché people as a site of meaning. In so doing, she also will explain and justify the political path that led a significant portion of the Mayan population to an armed insurrection in the Guatemalan highlands.

Chronicling the way of life of her people, Rigoberta Menchú intends to leave a record of a traditional system that has been violently voided of meaning. For her there is no clear epistemological distinction between scientific history and foundational myth, between narrative flow and documented fact, and consequently between ideal situations and real projects. She does not feel compelled to be "scientific"—a western concept of relative youth and doubtful meaning, according to post-modern literature. Rather, she weaves a symbolic representation of her people as she wants this story to be recorded in a projected and hypothetical posterity. Like nineteenth-century Latin American writers, Rigoberta Menchú is encouraged to fill in the gaps that the non-science of history leaves open. To fill in the gaps would help establish the legitimacy of the emerging "newly Mayanized Guatemala." The opportunity to direct that narrative toward a future ideal motivates her.

Because of this, her personal history does not really matter to her as it might to a Westerner trying to aggrandize him/herself. She is uninterested in speaking in an individualized way. She does not fully conceive of herself as an actor in this drama. She is merely the voice that narrates the story of a people. However, she frames the character within a particular cosmological set in which we are supposed to interpret allegories of public life that Mayan society wants us to understand. In these, the community as a whole stands at the center instead of the individual.

When Rigoberta Menchú was forced to leave Guatemala and resettle in Mexico City (1981), she was unknown in her own country or even among most Mayan people. Nationally, the name of Vicente Menchú, her father,[3] gained symbolic notoriety after the destruction of the Spanish Embassy by the Guatemalan Army.[4] A year later, an organization called Vicente Menchú Christian Revolutionaries was created. It soon became part of the "January 31st Popular Front," an umbrella group that included the CUC, labor groups and other popular organizations representing different segments of Guatemalan society. However, the ensuing urban military offensive, the purpose of which was to destroy what the military considered the rearguard of the revolutionary movement and its safehouses in the city, crushed most of these organizations in the summer of 1981. By the end of 1983 there was no trace left of the January 31st Popular Front. Of the organizations that were a part of it, only the CUC survives to this day.

Rigoberta Menchú had no claim to fame at the end of 1980. She was the daughter of a well-known Mayan grass-roots activist who was a martyr at the Spanish Embassy massacre. She was herself a member of the CUC and agitated on its behalf in Mexico City. In its desire to gain international recognition, the Guatemalan opposition to the military dictatorship launched a media blitz during 1981. Various representatives of different organizations living in Mexico toured the United States and Europe to convey the message of the Guatemalan struggle as well as of the ruthlessness and viciousness of its army. Menchú was chosen to go to Europe because of the implications of the Spanish embassy incident.

It was during this tour that Arturo Taracena, the Guatemalan representative of the movement in France, noticed her virtues as an articulate spokesperson. He asked anthropologist Elizabeth Burgos if she would be interested in exploring further the nature of Mayan society and their plight as a result of the army's policies. After she expressed interest, he arranged for a meeting between Menchú and Burgos. Both actors had to be pushed into the book project.[5] Rigoberta Menchú was not fully conscious at the time of the importance of doing such a testimonial, but together Taracena and the leadership of the CUC were able to convince her. Burgos had no expertise on Guatemala, but was very well connected to publishing houses through her ex-husband Regis Debray. Eventually the decision to tape Rigoberta Menchú's story was made. The process took place during the first weeks of 1982 at Burgos' house.

Subsequently, Burgos and Teracena in Paris, as well as members of CUC's leadership in Mexico were responsible for editing the book. Rigoberta Menchú has told Alice Brittin that at the time reading Spanish still was difficult for her. Therefore, other people had to read to her virtually the entire manuscript. Both she and the others deleted "things that spilled out of my mouth and it was necessary to take them out" (Brittin 1992: 11-12). Brittin goes on to observe that

> The Intervention of Solidarity organizations, Arturo Tercena and the CUC in the compilation of *Me llamo Rigoberta Menchú* confirms the obvious political bias of this *testimonio* and explains, in part, the politically charged level of discourse prevalent throughout the text. . . . However, as Rigoberta admits, what most inspired her to make public her story was the opportunity to share the "memory" of her life in hopes that it would not be forgotten like so many others. (Brittin 1993: 15)

The edited manuscript was presented by Burgos to the Casa de las Americas Contest, where it won the award as best testimonial narrative for 1983. That was the beginning of Rigoberta Menchú's international notoriety.

The book launched her as an international champion for human rights. Twelve years later, Menchú is a Nobel Peace Prize winner, a player within the global arena, adored by some, attacked by others. Her role as a living icon and a spokesperson for all Mayan peoples has succeeded where the Highlands insurrection did not. It has given a voice to the Mayans. It has given them new hope, new means of political enfranchisement and a new pride. All of this has expedited the merging of disparate Mayan groups within one unified political identity and brought them into a new political coalition.

Rigoberta Menchú has already played a significant political role both inside and outside of Guatemala's borders. She understands that her power is not personal nor individualistic but symbolic. It comes form what she represents for Guatemalans as the embodiment of other worldly ethical and moral purity in her quest for redemption of her people and pursuit of the cause initiated by her father, Vicente Menchú. It also comes from her ability to understand that the only way now left for all Guatemalan peoples, Mayan and non-Mayan, is to seek each other and deepen the democratic path, despite all its contradictions and stumbling blocks. She helps to pressure from below a racist state apparatus and a political class that will only be dismantled gradually, one step at a time.

In her movement from international floating signifier to concrete political actor, Rigoberta Menchú has succeeded in recasting a new identity over the ruins and fragments of other times, identities and spaces. Her memory was transposed onto the testimonial narrative as a strategy of resistance. It has succeeded in recasting her as a public figure, inserting her within Guatemala's national historical continuum. This is where she finds herself now. Mayan resistance is alive and has been revitalized. The main factor in this is her path from a peripheral silence to a verbal representation and self-constitution. This process re-territorializes a displaced identity, a space of subjectivity, that now allows her to participate in the empowerment of her own people, and in the transformation of the nation as a whole. Rigoberta Menchú's voice marks the coming of a new epoch in which Mayans and other marginalized Guatemalans repossess the conscience of past traumas to forge ahead with a new dynamism and new strategies of action.

This process has ethical and moral implications. It is these implications that Judith Thorn explores in *The Lived Horizon of My Being*. She is not so much interested in participating in an ongoing debate about the relationship between Guatemala's Mayas and the state nor contextualizing the Mayas participation during the Highlands insurrection. Rather, it is the moral underpinnings of Menchú's thought which obsess her and how these can be transformed into a particular *praxis*: how an individual can metamorphose him/herself on the basis of a set of ethical principles. This is her major contribution and it is *not* an insignificant one.

The difficulty of this enterprise is daunting, given the distance between both women. One, an academic writing from a Bakhtinian theoretical framework in the Bay Area. The other, coming from a marginal mountainous area within the Quiché itself. The bridge between them is the early texts of Mikhail Bakhtin.

Mikhail Bakhtin (b. Orel, 1895; d. Moscow, 1975) has become one of the leading cultural critics of the twentieth century. He wrote most of his work during the 1920s and 1930s, yet he remained relatively unknown to the outside world because he never published any of his manuscripts after 1929, when Stalin's dictatorship in the former Soviet Union became total. In fact, though arrested himself, he managed to survive by spending those long decades in exile in Kasakhstan. It was only during Kruschev's thaw that he finally returned to Moscow and gradually saw the reprinting of his major works. However, all of his early endeavors were still unpublished at his death. Not until 1979 were they published in Russia.

Bakhtin's contribution originates from a new understanding of the place of alterity in the interpretive experience. He claims that understanding is dialogical and that the aim of dialogue is not to unify, nor to integrate *self* and *other*, but rather to respect differences. In other words, the issue of otherness is the center of Bakhtin's theory.

Understanding, according to him, can never happen from the point of view of the *self*, but only from within the position of the *other*. What he implies by this is that we cannot come to a process of understanding ourselves, except through a perspective which comes from outside. That is why the spoken word, the living word uttered as actual speech, comes first. Utterances can convey meanings, living impulses that place the speakers in a particular and unique social environment. This means that the best model of human experience is a conversation. Its aim, however, is not to reach a synthesis, but rather to enlarge our own particular consciousness through our interaction with others.

To understand ourselves as subjects, however, becomes meaningless if we do not behave in an ethical way. The process of understanding ourselves and others implies a process of transformation of our own behavior towards others. This process will inevitably change us. This transformation can only happen from a sense of *self* and the sense of *self* can only come from our understanding of *otherness*.

In still tentative fashion, Bakhtin drew many of these conclusions in two of his lesser known early works, *Toward a Philosophy of the Act* (first English edition, 1993) and *Art and Answerability* (first English edition, 1990). These texts, originally written between 1917 and 1924, attempt to disclose an ethical interaction for modern human beings. Through dialogical interaction, a subject transforms him/herself, becomes a self-created subject, thus defeating selfish individuality. To be a valid subject, our lives have to have meaning. To have meaning, we as individuals have to express intentionality and purpose. The latter can only happen if we engage socially with others, recognize them, respond to them, debate with them. In this process we reach temporary truths as we continue a never-ending process of personal transformation that is the result of the continuous interaction with others around us. The subject, thus, is always a temporary stage in which elements of his/her own voice interact with elements of the voices of many other subjects, kaleidoscope-like, in a process of seeking personal responsibility and accountability.

Bakhtin's own early texts pointed to the relationship between philosophy and literary theory, and particularly the relation of aesthetics and ethics. However, he never tested his own theories on living situations. Scarred by Stalinism, he displaced these early intuitions to strict literary analysis and limited his *modus operandi* to the relations among the dialogizing characters of Dostoyevsky's novels. It has been left to Judith Thorn to test these possibilities by examining the self-constitution of a living subject with which she is creatively dialogizing from one foreign culture to another in order to come to terms with the depths of individual self-transformation and ethical responsibility and accountability. Here lies the originality of her own work.

To further explore the validity of her assumptions, Thorn also applies her methodology to the work of a Guatemalan writer of Mayan origin, Víctor Montejo (b. Jacaltenango, 1951). Montejo narrated his own near-death experience at the hands of the Guatemalan military in his book *Testimony: Death of a Guatemalan Village* (1987). An accomplished writer, he also has published a book of Mayan legends, *The Bird Who Cleans The World* (1993), a second testimonial about the destruction of Mayan lands at the hands of the military which so far has appeared only in Spanish; *Brevísima Relación Testimonial de la Destrucción del Mayab* (1992); and a bilingual book of poems, *Piedras Labradas* (1995). However, Thorn's analysis focuses on his first books, *Testimony: Death of a Guatemalan Village* and *El Kanil, Man of Lightning* (1984).

A short, little-known book, published bilingually a few years after Montejo's arrival in the United States, *El Kanil* centers its discourse on the nature of Mayan identity as different from, though in touch with, "Guatemalanness". Montejo's book is a reaction to the Guatemalan guerrillas' claim that they were waging war in the name of the Mayas, oppressed and discriminated by the Guatemalan ruling *Ladino*.[6] Still, Mayan voices are seldom heard when guerrillas articulate their own positions. Besides, *Ladinos* virtually monopolize all top positions in their own chain-of-command. However, the army "reads" this war as a war of *Ladinos* vs. Mayans—the result of guerrilla rhetoric—and reacts accordingly. The war is directly responsible for the destruction of Montejo's village, where he worked as one of very few Mayan school teachers available in the country, and it nearly cost him his own life. Montejo was interrogated by the military, but was finally released. He immediately fled to Mexico as a refugee. This bitter and scary experience leads to a literary-symbolic meditation about the nature of Mayan identity, about the nature of *otherness*, and about how one's identity can so easily be usurped and stripped of any meaningful connotations when you fail to name yourself through your writing or else by empowering your own public voice. These considerations, woven as a literary texture within the *bildungsroman* nature of *El K'anil*, echo those of Menchú. Both are uttered from within the Mayan spectrum, but for the difference that Menchú is then a semi-literate Quiché peasant, whereas Montejo is a Jacaltec school teacher and writer. As a result, they complement each other in their concerns and in the source of their reflection abut the nature of their own identity and about the metamorphosis of the *self*, despite their cultural and class differences.

Thorn's writing is by no means perfect. As with many first books, she is still searching in the dark for certainties that will never be found. In these processes she happily contradicts herself, essentializing Mayan identities that she has posited as in permanent flux, at times romanticizing the linear behavior of her subjects of study. Occasionally, she will charge like Don Quixote against the windmills of critical theory that deny a voice to the subjects of her devotion and allegiance. Thorn takes her desires for reality. Here and there the style can be turgid, condensed and charged. It is not an easy book to read. Its assertiveness and earnestness can betray either a narrow perspective or else put in evidence the clear pursuit of a vision, strongly intuited if not wholly coalesced as yet in a new theoretical viewpoint.

It is her moral concern that makes it unique as a way of coming to terms with the paramount meaning of testimonial literature. This singular perspective connects academic/literary questions with moral/ethical issues. No published work that I know of has done this. In the process, she displays great knowledge and familiarity with contemporary critical thinking. However, this is not for the purpose of hiding behind the insufferable mask of certain fashionable theories that merely drop names and fake it with opaque language games. Theoretical gestures like those simply obscure and dissipate the works that they purportedly analyze, since what is on display is not a genuine quest for knowledge but the fireworks and fanfare of the juggler's acts.

In Thorn's case there is honest mud-wrestling with her subject. She betrays love and respect for the voices she is dealing with, and takes their meanings awfully seriously. She wants them to be treated earnestly as well, not as orphaned, disenfranchised subjects begging for attention in the canonic streets of Eurocentric Literary legitimacy. She resents their being discriminated or brought down a peg because of their ethnic origins, validates the subaltern subject and wants his/her voice heard on all center-periphery relationships. This attitude is most commendable. It also brings her own effort closer to the legitimacy of success than to the dignity of failure.

Even in the most obscure passages, we can see and feel and hear Thorn's mind at work. We can only hope that her research will contribute to a new examination of ethics as the underpinning of human behavior. Surprisingly, outside of traditional philosophy, ethics remain to this day one of the most under-explored dimensions of culture.

ARTURO ARIAS
San Francisco, 1996

Foreword Endnotes

[1] The Quiché people constitute the largest of all the Maya-speaking groups, comprising a total population of over one million people. Approximately 20 more Maya speaking groups survive to this day in Mexico and Guatemala. The original translation of the *Popol-Vuh* from Quiché to Spanish by Dominican friar Francisco Ximénez, written in 1724, is located at the Newberry Library in Chicago. The best English translation is provided by Dennis Tedlock (Touchstone Books, 1985). The authors of the *Popol-Vuh* claim they wrote it because "the original book" is "now lost." Still unknown to this day: What happened to the original book used by Ximénez to copy his own version and was there an original text destroyed by the Spanish conquistadors.

[2] Fed up with abuses and exploitation, a significant number of Mayans joined left-wing guerrillas in an insurrection against the military dictatorship in power since 1954. The army responded with brutality reminiscent of Nazi atrocities. By their own admission, they razed over 450 villages during their scorched-earth campaign of 1981-1982. *The New York Times* estimates that approximately 110,000 people were killed during this period. Approximately half-a-million more fled to the safety of Mexico.

[3] A devout Christian, Vicente Menchú was one of the founders of the Committee for Peasant Unity (CUC, in Spanish) in the early 1970s. CUC had a radical Christian orientation and was constituted mainly by Mayan peasants from the Central and North-Central highlands of the country.

[4] The Guatemalan Army deliberately set fire to the Spanish embassy in Guatemala City—against the expressed will of the Spanish government—on January 31, 1980, in order to prevent a press conference denouncing human rights violations in the Quiché region. Twenty-seven CUC militants were burned alive along with embassy personnel and ordinary people seeking visas. Among its victims were Vicente Menchú, Rigoberta's father. Everybody died except for the ambassador who jumped from the flaming roof, and a Mayan man rescued with third-degree burns. He was subsequently kidnapped from the hospital by an army death squad and mutilated to death. Subsequently, Spain broke diplomatic relations with Guatemala.

[5] Alice Brittin, "Close Encounters of the Third World Kind: Rigoberta Menchú and Elizabeth Burgos, *Me llamo Rigoberta Menchú*" (1993: 10).

[6] *Ladino* is a Guatemalan term synonymous with *mestizo*. *Ladinos* are people of mixed Mayan and Spanish blood with a clearly Western, modernizing outlook.

Preface
and
Acknowledgments

My first debt of gratitude is to Dr. Vadim Liapunov and the University of Texas Press, without whom this manuscript could not have been written. In 1990, as I read *The Dialogic Imagination*, I became convinced that Mikhail Mikhailovich Bakhtin (1895-1975), who authored those extraordinary essays, must have written something of a general philosophical nature—a treatise on the human condition—based on ethics rather than Marxist theory, which provided the groundwork for his later work. Dr. Caryl Emerson referred me to Dr. Liapunov, whose translation of *Toward a Philosophy of the Act* was in its draft stages for the University of Texas Press. The correlation between *Toward a Philosophy of the Act* and my study of the literature of Guatemala became what Bakhtin refers to as "my participative non-alibi in being."

Bakhtin came to me as a surprise. I fought with his words, and yet I agreed with what he said. In the video which runs incessantly in my mind, I imagine him in the cold, with one leg, wearing a green velvet jacket, full of holes, dictating to his wife, who is loyal and bored. I see him meeting Rigoberta Menchú, who stands at his door, barefoot in the snow in her *huipil*. I hear them talking about the Diaspora and exile. He invites her in without asking why she is there. Bakhtin offers to show Menchú his writing. She says she cannot read. He realizes he smoked up his manuscript when he needed cigarette papers. They are enchanted and puzzled with each other. "How can people and places be so different and yet so similar?" they wonder. Theory and life together create praxis.

I am molded by the lives of others, but most especially I have been touched by the humanness of the life of Rigoberta Menchú who, as an almost complete stranger, has lived with me in my mind and heart. I recognize in *Me llamo Rigoberta Menchú* a process which I have lived, under different and less tragic circumstances.

More immanently, because they have been so near me in the flesh, are three individuals who have shared important parts of their lives with me: my son Jesse, whom I have watched with amazement for fifteen years; my friend Steven López, who, to use the words of Reynaldo Arenas, "conspired not against tyranny but for life" with AIDS; and

Roberto Rivera, who, with his dignified heart, is my colleague, my teacher and my friend.

But that is not all. I am surrounded by many other friends without whom nothing in my life would seem as possible. Three of these individuals are Christine Cariati; Cliff Gerrish, who designed the cover of this book; and Erika Bliss, who helped me proof. Evelyn Smith de Gálvez, my publisher, has become my friend while endeavoring to contain my commas and dependent clauses. So, if I had my way, this book would be a gift from all of us, named and unnamed. But I would take responsibility for all the *picados*, omissions and commissions.

I am honored by Arturo Arias' frankness about my work since all our statements are tentative attempts to organize meaning. His understanding of the intent behind the words on these pages makes him a friend of my mind.

Thank you, Víctor Montejo, for your bravery, your friendship and the poetry of *El Kanil*.

JUDITH THORN
San Francisco, 1996

interlocutors. The combination of the works by Menchú and Montejo provides us with a viewpoint, a sentient historicity, a delineation of the Mayan world and their experience of being Maya. The books are also about being *other* in two worlds.

Me llamo Rigoberta Menchú, *Testimony: Death of a Guatemalan Village*, and *El Kanil: Man of Lightning* are bound together by certain elements. The first and most significant is that the individual speakers and their narratives express and describe an hermeneutical process[3] whose theme is self-fulfillment and reconciliation. This process includes:

1. The absorption/internalization of outside, generally prejudicial, opinion concerning the individual;[4]
2. Assessment of the *self*, relative to that outside influence, which is essential to reconciliation and situating one's *self* ideologically;
3. A metamorphosis that begins with a conscious volition to change;
4. The growth of a modulated and self-sustaining person, which represents a shift outward from moral and ethical contemplation and consideration to speech and individuation.
5. Finally, the projection of that *self* into the world at large, through praxis.[5]

The sense of *self*, which develops as a result of this process, is at once sovereign and interdependent, responsive to the world around it. It is both reflexive and reflective. The reconciliation manifests itself with respect to the past, the present world, the self, the land and culture, the outsider, and the means of expression and choice of language.

By recording fables and epics from oral history, narrating testimonials in addition to working in anthropology, literature and philosophy, these two individuals, Rigoberta Menchú and Víctor Montejo, articulate a cultural interaction which unites a popular viewpoint with an intellectual one. Even more, they join theoretical and functional discourse in praxis.

Bakhtin's early philosophical works, *Toward a Philosophy of the Act* and *The Author and Hero in Aesthetic Activity* provide the framework for my discussion on this journey of the self and birth of consciousness. Both offer a comprehensive and unifying theory not only of aesthetics, but also of politics, religion, mythology, love, and death, all treated from the standpoint of ethical responsibility.[6]

I have chosen to develop a dialogue of equals between the two Mayan writers, Menchú and Montejo, and Mikhail Mikhailovich Bakhtin because both he and they have come from divergent positions and have

Introduction

We have had to ask but little of the imagination,
for our crucial problem has been a lack of conventional means
to render our lives believable.

Miguel Angel Asturias

There are some individuals who because of intriguing and unusual
circumstances enter a discourse from below or from a peripheral position,
rise to prominence and thereby change the current of thinking about a
subject. For example, Malcom X and Ghandi were people who, because
of their dramatic life experiences, were able to understand and articulate
a transformative vision for the world as it existed in their era. Thereafter,
through their emotional and intellectual dedication to their ideals, they
were able to maintain their vision with messianic fervor, uniting theory
with action. For us as readers, a meeting with one of these individuals is
"a meeting with a great human being . . . something that determines,
obligates and unites—this is the highest moment of understanding." [1]

In our own age, Rigoberta Menchú is one of these individuals.
Menchú is Maya Quiché from San Miguel Uspantan, Guatemala. Her
reflection on her life, entitled *Me llamo Rigoberta Menchú, y así me nacio
la conciencia*,[2] is a narrative testimonial and spiritual ethnography,
literally a progress of the soul for her self and her people's cultural history.
Transcribed and edited by anthropologist Elisabeth Burgos-Debray, *Me
llamo Rigoberta Menchú, y así me nacio la conciencia* was awarded the
Casa de las Américas Prize. Rigoberta Menchú received the Nobel Prize
for Peace in 1992.

The Lived Horizon of My Being considers Rigoberta Menchú's life
within the context of her testimonial. The discussion of her work will be
supplemented by an analysis of a documentary testimonial, *Testimony:
Death in a Guatemalan Village*, transcribed by Víctor Montejo, Maya
from Jacaltenango, Guatemala. Montejo, an anthropologist who received
his Ph.D. from the University of Connecticut, has also transcribed and
written *El Kanil: Man of Lightning*, an epic from the oral literature of
Huehuetenango, a book of fables entitled *The Bird Who Cleans the World,*
and recently a book of poems translated by Víctor Perera. In 1992, he
published *Brevísima relación testimonial de la continua destrucción del
Mayab'* (A Brief Testimonial Account of the Continuing Destruction of
the Mayan People of Guatemala), with Q'anil Akab' and other Mayan

arrived at a most compatible center. In a sense, they meet me and I, them, through the process of cultural mediation. A space for cultural mediation can reduce the friction caused by unequal access to power, and presents Bakhtin and Menchú with equal availability, using their own words. Because the issue of voice (who gets to speak and for whom) is a pivotal issue in cultural studies, the body of the book uses the work of Mayan peasants and scholars to delineate Mayan culture. Although any quote is preempted from its original context, I am honoring Mayan sources, quoting them in depth, rather than using the writing of outsiders to describe Mayan reality. Bakhtin describes the intellectual component of the project which Menchú and Montejo understand through different levels of experience.[7] Because of this interaction, these two viewpoints can be said to speak to each other.

Bakhtin, Montejo and Menchú all perceive the continuum of the past into the future and the lack of polarities in life. All three describe a "both/and" rather than the "either/or" which is characteristic of a binary opposition. The three of them share a strong ethical sense, a belief in personal responsibility. They all have a sense of the epic past, an understanding that there is ideology behind every language we speak and a sense of and hope for the future. They share a similar understanding of the experience of pain and love as an unfettered act. They have a shared concept of *self/other* that is both independent and interdependent. All three value of the human being over the idea and see a dependence on praxis as the test of one's belief system. For each of them, the understanding of these things takes place through metamorphosis into a new and developing consciousness, rather than mimesis.

Finally, in both the text of Bakhtin and the life of Rigoberta Menchú and her dialogue with her culture, we can understand what Bakhtin calls the *lived horizon of being*, the fulfillment of the aesthetic experience. Bakhtin writes that what makes an action specifically aesthetic is an individual's inter-reaction to the whole of another person as a human being. For Rigoberta Menchú, this is her transformation, becoming *another other*, one whose *otherness* is defined on and in her own terms.

Parallels Between Bakhtin's Theory and the Development of the Testimonial

In order to explain the process of self-fulfillment and reconciliation, it is necessary to describe briefly the interrelation between M.M. Bakhtin's ideas about the development of discourse in the novel and how the development of the novel parallels the development of the testimonial and the *self.*

In a theory which he called *excess of seeing*, Bakhtin explains that what I see looking at an individual and what that individual sees of himself are not the same, As we gaze at each other two different worlds are reflected in the pupils of our eyes." [8] The result of this interdependent vision is a unique and irreplaceable event, because each individual sees and understands differently a given place or moment. This vision produces new kinds of knowledge and insights. Coming face to face with an alternative point of view, as we do in Rigoberta Menchú's testimony of her life, can provide for us the *excess of seeing* necessary for creative understanding and growth, which is the essence of the aesthetic experience, but only if we are willing to engage thereafter in a process of self-evaluation, which Bakhtin calls *objectification.*

Bakhtin tells us in *Philosophy of the Act* that *theorism* is a specific tendency in Western thinking that takes from concrete human examples and makes an abstraction from which a set of rules and norms is derived. The theoretical world exists as if the individual did not, even though modern philosophy does *know ethics and reason* (Bakhtin 1993). Because of this, contemporary philosophy is in a state of crisis. Although Bakhtin wrote these words early in his career, just after the Russian revolution, this crisis still manifests itself in what some call the *post-modern condition.* He writes, "*Being* itself is a phenomenological concept, a part of experience." When the content of an act or occurrence is broken away or separated from the event itself, the content becomes *culture* (an abstraction) and the event is robbed of its integrity. Individuals are not responsible to concepts, rather to the actions and repercussions of a *lived life.* In fact, one's entire life can be considered to be a single multifaceted action or deed. The philosophy which attempts to describe "*being* as event" must describe "not the world produced by that event, but the world in which that act becomes answerably aware of itself, and is performed" (Bakhtin 1993: 38).

At this point in his argumentation, Bakhtin compares a single individual's perception with the vast whole of knowledge. How can anything for which I am responsible make a difference? As we move from finite acts to the infinite we carry those acts with us. In an infinite regression, without a core of individual cognition and responsibility, there would be only vacant space and the system would collapse. He asks pointedly, "What if the very act of abstraction is the problem? What if the real phenomena occurring in the lived life are not reducible?" Obviously we need to begin again, looking at the concrete, the episode of life, the individual perception. "We attempt to incorporate our actual life into a possible, theoretical context, either by identifying as essential only the universal moments in our actual life, or by understanding it in the sense of its being a small scrap of the space and time of the large spatial and temporal whole, or by giving it symbolic interpretation" (Bakhtin 1993: 62).

"To express our *self*," Bakhtin writes, "means that we make our *self* an object for another to view." He calls this the *actualizing of consciousness*, the first step in *objectification*. Ultimately, as self-defined individuals we can reflect on our own selves as objects, and our discourse becomes the object we investigate (Bakhtin 1993). This is what Rigoberta Menchú and Víctor Montejo help us do. Menchú's lifework is corroborated by the tales and epics recorded by Víctor Montejo, and by her personal understanding of her cultural framework and experience. The specific context of Menchú, Montejo and the Maya of Guatemala will be discussed in the part two of this study.

Bakhtin, in his essay, "Forms of Time and Chronotope in the Novel,"[9] states that early forms of chronotope (orders of spatial and temporal time) were defined by hagiographic examples in *everyday type adventure*, in which the metamorphosis from sinful life to crisis to redemption and sainthood is foregrounded. A bit further on, Bakhtin divides the forms of chronotope in ancient Greece into two types. The first of these is autobiography, in which the individual passes through set stages of life, especially as seen in Socrates' records of the dialogues of Plato. There is a moment of crisis and rebirth, which, in the case of Plato himself, was his message from the oracle. A second Greek chronotope was rhetorical autobiography. These autobiographies were of real human beings making an oral and public account of themselves, as in the *agora*. Bakhtin points out that these speeches, which were the venue of the under classes, were not for personal aggrandizement.

> These forms were not works of a literary or bookish nature, kept aloof from the concrete social and political act of noisily making themselves public. On the contrary, these forms were completely determined by events: verbal praise of civil and political acts or real human beings giving accounts of themselves. (Bakhtin 1981: 131)

However, Bakhtin relates that in the eras that followed, these venues were eradicated by the rise of the nation state and the resulting manifestations of class and power. "Man's image was distorted by his increasing participation in the mute and invisible spheres of existence. He was literally drenched in muteness and invisibility. And with them entered loneliness. The personal and detached human being—'the man who exists for himself'—lost the unity and wholeness that had been a product of his public origin" (Bakhtin 1981: 135).

The early chronotopes depicted by Bakhtin parallel the development of narrative texts themselves from epic to novel and are related to the development of the characters in novelistic discourse. They also parallel the development of the *self* in Rigoberta Menchú's testimonial. The events she describes in her testimonial prefigure the articulation of the *self* in the same way that Bakhtin's Greek chronotopes are precursors of the time frame in the modern novel. These stages also parallel the development of the *self*. The sense of self-worth moves from the solely public sphere, which is externally dependent, to an understanding of the relation of that self to the outside world. The *authoring* of the self, the *substantiation* of the self and finally the *projection* of the self into the world are the critical stages of an ethical and articulated being, which is both interdependent and independent.

As Bakhtin works through his chronotopes into his theory on the development of the novel,[10] he envisions the novel as an aesthetic act which is a new form for expressing time's fullness, a form relating to the uncovering of social contradictions on a most basic level. This uncovering of contradictions is the root of consciousness (Bakhtin 1981). Once an event is portrayed on the same "time-value plane" as that of living beings, the world of the novel begins. Bakhtin links the novel with a multi-languaged consciousness and a radical change effected within the temporal coordinates of the literary image. His temporal coordinates comprise the use of the present as context, the consciousness of the relativity of the past and a concrete sense of the future. These aspects of novelistic development delineate a progression similar to the process of reconciliation in the testimonial of Rigoberta Menchú. What Bakhtin describes is a process of textual or historical development as well:

> The literary artistic consciousness of the modern novel, sensing itself on the border between two languages, one literary and the other extra literary, each of which now knows heteroglossia, also senses itself on the border of time: it is extraordinarily sensitive to time in language. (Bakhtin 1981: 67)

These interactions between languages could occur only when there were dramatic contacts with other groups of people, especially during periods of developing nationalism, imperialism or colonization. One could conclude, then, that the authorship of the *self* and the development of the character in the novel could occur only after the development of the possibility that an independent self existed, not just an externally dependent individual. The concept of agency came into being only after the Renaissance and the Age of Enlightenment in Europe, confirmed and provoked by science, religion and navigation.

The novel itself provided the needed cohesive element in allowing readers to 'see' areas of life from which they have become separated because of class distinctions. The novel, as textual production, also served to validate the national epic past and folklore, and to project the specific national configuration outward. This in turn changed the idea the nation's inhabitants themselves had about who they were. The novel reflected the process by which nationalism began to codify, enhance and stabilize itself. We can see in the works of both Rigoberta Menchú and Víctor Montejo the process which produces a canon of national literature for international consumption.

Although contemporary scholars have written that the nature of the novel is colonial and discursively oppressive, we will see, in the work of these two speakers, how the tools that were developed as a means of oppression are used by the oppressed to forge or obtain liberation. Mary Louise Pratt calls the appropriation of the tools of the other *transculturation*, a concept that derives from the Cuban writer, Fernando Ortiz. In her book *Imperial Eyes*, Pratt details the characteristics of ethnobiography and autobiography (in the form of slave narratives):

> [O]ften facilitated by dissident western intellectuals . . . self-descriptions structured to a degree, in line with western literary institutions and western conceptions of culture and the self, yet in direct opposition to official ideologies of colonialism and slavery . . . these early texts undertook not to reproduce but to engage western discourses of identity, community, selfhood and otherness. . . . When such autoethnographic texts are read simply as "authentic" self-expression or "unauthentic assimilation," their transcultural character is obliterated and their dialogic engagement with western modes of representation is lost.[11]

In Bakhtin's theoretical constructions, the testimonial of Rigoberta Menchú is an *actualizing of consciousness* because she makes of herself an object to be viewed. The testimonial could also be called a chronotope. In *Forms of Chronotope in the Novel*, Bakhtin writes:

> The chronotope is the place where the knots of narrative are tied and untied. It can be said that to them belongs the meaning that shapes narrative. . . . We cannot but be impressed by the representational importance of the chronotope. . . . Chronotopes are mutually inclusive, they co-exist, they may be interwoven with, replace or oppose one another, contradict one another or find themselves in ever more complex interrelationships. The relationships that exist among chronotopes cannot enter into any of the relationships contained within chronotopes. (Bakhtin 1981: 248-53)

Especially in the case of Montejo and Menchú, the testimonial is political, meant to apply pressure and increase understanding. Inasmuch as the chronotope is a distillation of the place and time of an event of a human life, it must remain inviolate. "Out of the actual chronotopes of our world (which serve as the source of representation) emerge the reflected and created chronotopes of the world represented in the text" (Bakhtin 1981: 253). The testimonial could not have occurred without the super-availability of advanced technology which also allows a person to access and appropriate it without being party to the hegemonic power which produced it. Testimonials are counter discursive, even though all of them are not as complex or riveting as Menchú's. The difference is the process that she describes and lives, which is the reason for this study.

Bakhtin, in celebrating the diversity of the speech act itself, shows that it is necessary to define the *self*, because that definition gives meaning to the group. The differences we see in others can be used to define ourselves. Bakhtin writes, "The artist's struggle to achieve a determinate and stable image of the hero is to a considerable extent a struggle with himself."[12]

In later essays, especially "The Bildungsroman," Bakhtin reiterates his early theory. He describes two sub-categories of the novel that are pertinent to this discussion. (In Bakhtin's discussions, novelistic elements can be either fictive or life events.) The first is the novel of ordeal. The plot of this novel is always "constructed on the deviations from the normal course of the author's life, exceptional events and situations that would not be found in the typical normal ordinary biography" (Bakhtin 1986: 14). The world is not capable of changing the hero, it only tests him. This is *not* Rigoberta Menchú, for the essence of her testimonial is not only the tests she endured but more importantly the changes which were brought about in her, as a result. "Rather," Bakhtin stated, "there is an incomparably rarer type of novel that provides an image of [wo]man in the process of becoming" (Bakhtin 1986: 23). In it, changes in the hero acquire plot significance. This type of novel can be designated as "the novel of human emergence. . . . Human emergence is of quite a different nature. It is no longer man's own private affair. He emerges along with the world and he reflects the historical emergence of the world itself" [read feminine gender here] (Bakhtin 1986: 23). In order for Rigoberta Menchú to come from her oral tradition to the position that she now holds, it was necessary for her to pass through the stages that Bakhtin outlines, going from oral tradition to textuality, from an ancient position similar to the one developed in the Greek chronotope of the *agora*, to one which is indicative of the modern novel. We shall see these processes occurring in the testimonial.[13] Briefly, according to the Casa de las Américas:

> A *testimonio* must document some aspect of Latin American or Caribbean reality from a direct source. A direct source is understood as a knowledge of the facts by the author or his or her compilation of narratives or evidence obtained from the individuals involved or qualified as witnesses. In both cases reliable documentation, written or graphic, is indispensable. The form is at the author's discretion, but literary quality is also indispensable.[14]

A testimonial is both a bridge and a vehicle. It is not just confessional self-accounting, nor is it only a reflection of the "me as understood by others." The testimonial derives from an ageless oral tradition of witnessing and reportage. Rigoberta Menchú states in her narrative that her ancestors bore testimony to what they witnessed. "They don't tell them the way that it's written down in books, because the majority of Indians can't read and write, and don't even know that they have their own texts. No, they learn it through oral recommendations, the way it has been handed down through the generations" (Menchú 1984: 13).

As a newly developing genre, it has provided a more flexible space for voices which have not or would not otherwise be heard, because of problems of language and literacy and access. The testimonial can be especially valuable for women as narrators because they have even less access to education than men. Testimonials provide a venue of expression for non-traditional writers; therefore, they are part of the literary process which exists outside the mainstream of traditional literary work. Perhaps because they have a less-familiar construction, the style appears more genuine, more raw or closer to its source. In the context of life events they are indeed more genuine. Because they are based on life events, there is an inter-relationship here between form and content. The genre itself is still a developing form and takes on a myriad of styles and variations. Some are called narrative, testimonial fiction, ethno-fiction, ethnobiography, novella-testimonial, or testimonial novel, depending on reflected purpose. There are numerous expositions on testimonial literature, especially the work of Marc Zimmermann, John Beverley and Elzbieta Sklowdowska.

The form of the testimonial resembles under-class memoirs, centered on episodes or a single incident in an individual's life. These statements are often politically motivated and edited and elaborated by editors who have sufficient literary skills to produce a cohesive text. For Bakhtin, form cannot be understood independently of content. He writes:

> No artistic genre can organize itself around suspense alone. . . . Only a human life, or at least something directly touching it, is capable of evoking such suspense. This human factor must be revealed in some substantial aspect . . . it must possess a sense of *living reality*. (Bakhtin 1981: 107)

Me llamo Rigoberta Menchú and *Testimony: Death of a Guatemalan Village* are by heroic people about the heroism of the common individual. Today, Rigoberta Menchú also bears witness with Víctor Montejo, to the voyage of their reality, word/story into the non-Mayan world.

Part One

Text in Context:
The Interanimation of Theory and Lived Life

In order to develop an adequate understanding of the context of the two testimonials which are considered in this manuscript, we will investigate briefly the external considerations that affect the process of self-substantiation within the categories described in the introduction.

Absorption/Internalization of External Opinion

Historically, in and outside of Guatemala, the *voice* of the Mayan people has been mute or muted by outside circumstances. These circumstances have induced the emotional exile inherent in colonial subjugation and conquest, which Octavio Paz, in writing about Mexico, called *psychic diaspora*. Since the first encounters of the 'old' world with the 'new', indigenous people of the Americas have been characterized by negation, affirming the anxieties of their oppressors. These litanies began with Cristóbal Colón, who called the inhabitants of the new world *savages*. Later, Diego de Landa and others called them *idolators* and *murderers*. Their written documents established the beginning of colonial discourse on the Americas, which became the basis of rationalization for the abuses of power that came thereafter. Subsequent conclusions about the cultural practice of the inhabitants of the new world were based on observations, but they were discolored by projections and assumptions.

Colonial discourse, which occurs on a geographical and ideological plane, is a linguistically based practice that includes ways of writing and speaking *about* a subject. Large amounts of textual material and chronicles of deeds and conquests were produced for Europeans through a process that used sets of criteria, methods and analysis not available or valid or known in the territory of those who were the subjects of these documents. Ultimately the discourse separated itself from the people who were its subjects.[15] It resulted in paternalism, as well as economic, social and political domination.

At the time of the Spanish Conquest there were at least two Mayan language systems: glyphs on public buildings and Mayan books, which were talking books comprised of pictures with glyphs and/or oral interpretations. In the Viceroyalty of Guatemala, *auto de fe's* (massive book burnings) sponsored by Diego de Landa and other priests who came with the conquistadors to evangelize, resulted in the obliteration of that literacy in the indigenous people and cleared the way for the implanting of Spanish and cursive/alphabet writing in Meso America. De Landa proselytized and eradicated primarily amongst the aristocracy because he misunderstood the interconnections between the calendric and social order, assuming, it seems, that the Mayan order of hierarchy had the same functions as those with which he was familiar. In ancient times the interaction between social performance and the calendar proceeded through different levels, each with its own use. The nobles and families were influenced by calendars in three operating systems: long count, based on 52 (weeks); lunar, the sacred calendar based on gestation for agriculture and reproduction; and solar, based on astronomy and the rotation of the earth. What remained behind—in this specific case, following De Landa's destruction of the aristocracy—and which exists to this day are complex readings of the agricultural calendar. Yucatec-speaking Mayan peasants fled and were found in the *selva lacandona* in Chiapas hundreds of years after the Conquest by missionaries who recognized their language and requested interpreters. Having obliterated their texts and those who could interpret them, the colonial process preemptively denigrated the colonized as inferior because the colonized had no written language, further reinforcing the European notion that those who cannot write are innately inferior to those who can. The colonized could then be objectified in the eyes of those with power.

There was no immediate way to reclaim 'voice' in the context of the power that had negated its existence. In a literal and metaphoric way these Mayan groups were left with their tongues intact. But, deprived of an outside *other* who could hear them, these tongues became as mute to the outside world as the stones on which the glyphs were carved. It has now become politically important for those who are the objects of colonial discourse, in this case the Maya, to undermine claims made by those outside powers to see what was concealed and how they as the colonized were affected by the colonial process. It is significant that within this assessment is a reconsideration of the spiritual aspects of the ancient calendar system and a revitalization of Mayan spirituality.

Paulo Freire refers to the milieu of the oppressed (those who became the subjects of these discursive practices) as the *culture of silence*. This silence and oppression is the theme of *Testimony: Death of a Guatemalan Village*. It is a primary theme in *Me llamo Rigoberta Menchú*. The context of and catalyst for these two testimonials is institutionalized violence and the systematic attempted destruction of the cultural cohesion of the indigenous people of Guatemala. The contemporary incursion of the military into the lives of those people, whether as a response to the progressive ideas among the Maya or as a result of an independent desire on the part of non-indigenous people to maintain Mayan subordination in any of its manifestations, has affected this process.[16] In these testimonials, personal freedom and physical emancipation are inexorably interwoven.

Whereas repression and domination, whether political or socioeconomic, often destroy the will to resist, this has not always been the case with the Mayan people. Domination/subordination has not diminished the sense of ethnic identity or cultural continuity. Arturo Arias, discussing *El Norte* (1991), described ethnicity as that which

> characterizes a population whose members self-define their collective survival by a shared identity through cultural and biological self-reproduction. For this particular purpose they share a myth of origin, which brings forth nostalgic remnants of a collective past and a common origin. As a result, contextual elements of tradition, popular rites and communal lifestyle translate into a kind of timeless mythic imagery.

But culture and language, as an integral part of culture, are marginal to external power and are threatened by it. Maintenance of a lifestyle in keeping with a continuity of cultural traditions is a strong theme in all the work discussed here. Language and ethnic identity are inherent parts of this process. Enrique Sam Colop, a Maya Quiché poet and scholar, called for the socio-political recognition of a Mayan *nation* in 1988, based on the fact that the Maya have an ethnic consciousness of themselves, even though they represent diverse language groups.[17]

It is a testimony to the strength of the Mayan cultural tradition that under the duress of outside forces, traditional foundations of indigenous life have not only survived but flourished, even as 'modernity' in some of its forms is being adopted.[18] Maya are not looking to become 'Western' or assimilated into *Ladino* culture, although the products of modern technology are being effectively used by them to promote their cause as well as enhance the quality of their lives. George Yudice writes: "Paradoxically, modernity in Latin America is more a question of establishing new relationships with tradition than of surpassing it."[19] The Maya do not unilaterally acknowledge that overt cultural modification—for example not wearing *traje*, especially among men in some communities, used by some to indicate *Ladinization*—has had a deleterious effect on their ethnic identity or their lives. At the same time *traje* bears a special significance. Menchú wrote in 1992:

Todo eso son tragedias en la vida de la gente, pero la otra parte de la reacción es lo alegre que es la obra que hace la gente, o sea los huipiles, todos los huipiles tienen una ternura, una expresión . . . es decir era como un escape para expresar una alegría de la naturaleza, de la vida y de todo un pueblo silenciado que habla a través de su obra. Quién sabe, debieran ser nuestros huipiles tan tristes y tan pobres si de veras la gente reflejara en ellos solo su dolor y no es su dolor, es realmente la combinación de sueños, de ilusiones, es decir la vida continua con mucha fuerza. (Menchú 1992: n.p.)

[All of these are tragedies in the life of the people; but the other side is how joyful are the works of art that the people make. In other words, the *huipiles* possess a tenderness and an expression. It is a way of expressing a joy about nature and about life, about a silenced people who speak through their handicraft. Our *huipiles* would be so sad and poor if people only reflected their pain. But it is not pain. It is really a combination of dreams, illusions, and the continuing life-force. That is to say life continues with great vitality.]

In one way or another, most Mayan people believe that to remain resistant to change is unrealistic. They are 'prudent', changing to avoid exploitation, choosing things that they believe will enhance their lives, and thoughtful about the course of events. To do otherwise would be to die at their own hand. They would have in fact become their own oppressors, destroyed by atrophy and inertia.[20] The interaction of cultures reinforces those patterns that are useful and allows for the evolution of a people as a living organism. Whatever touches us, changes us.

In *The Guatemalan Indians and the State*, Arturo Arias writes about cultural upheaval and change as well as the encroachment of Western commodity culture. According to Arias, indigenous identity was transformed primarily by the installation of the cargo system because its intricacies worked themselves out as a zero sum proposition; the reliance on external funds and fertilizers; the increase of external exchange in other indigenous and non-indigenous communities, caused by the fragmenting of the *milpa* system to provide room for cash crops; Catholic Action; and finally, the earthquake of 1976 that left millions homeless and desperately impoverished.

We, as outsiders, now see the Maya, as a unified people. After 500 years of oppression, they have no way to conjecture—nor do we—what they would have been if they had been otherwise free from the constraints and projections of colonial practices.

Assessment of Self-Consideration of and Reconciliation with Outside Opinion, Ideology, Language, and Culture

> Everything that pertains to me enters my consciousness, beginning with my name, from the external world through the mouths of others with their intonation, in their emotional and value assigning tonality. I realize myself initially through others. Just as the body is formed initially in the mother's womb, a person's consciousness awakens wrapped in another's consciousness.
>
> M.M. Bakhtin, *Speech Genres and Other Late Essays*

The process of reconciliation and self-fulfillment necessitates corrective inquiry into the historical aspects of the problem. How did we come to be in this place? This is truly anamnesis—a working-through of origins rather than a repression of them.[21]

All systems change because of external force impressed upon them. In the Western world, our writing is about leaving a trace. In other places, *costumbre* (cultural signifier) exists in the forms of myth and ritual contacts, and contracts of kinship, hairstyles, *traje* (regional clothing), tools, ornaments, assignment of roles, divisions of labor, as well as perceived organization of the natural world through myth and reality. All of these things are transferred through memory and by consequent behavior, as ways people use consistently to identify themselves to one another and separate themselves from others.

> Ethnic identity had been transformed in the search for political force. Now, identity was a tangible, verbalized phenomenon around which the articulation of political practices was sought. But the symbolic practices, the world view and the unconscious codes had been discarded without the formation of new ones to substitute for them. Thus, in concrete practice, just as identity was being talked about more openly, it was experiencing its deepest crisis. (Arias 1992: 251)

Víctor Montejo writes that the reign of terror of the military affected indigenous people by undermining the growing consciousness of cultural identity; attempting to stop the politicization of the native people of Guatemala, especially the education of the *Indian* and those overwhelmingly exploited on plantations; and attempting to destroy the unification of the Maya as a people because it is a threat to the bourgeoisie.[22]

The Mayan people understand the need for education. The first conference on Mayan education was held in Quetzaltenango in July of 1994. A keynote speaker for the conference was Víctor Montejo, who reminded those present of the destruction of books that preceded the physical conquest of the Mayan people. The assessment of Mayan educational practices, he said, proceeds on many levels from "mitos y la espiritualidad, a La espiritualidad, a escritura simbólica y numérica, el trabajo, y adaptación tecnológica."[23]

The Mayan people have been resilient in their dedication to their mother tongues. In fact, Nora England reports that language difference is seen by Mayans as the "only *true* non-*Ladino* trait."[24] Margarita López Raquec, a Mayan anthropologist, says: "El idioma (Kaqchikel) constituye definitivamente un bastión ineludible, que apoyará otros campos de acción. Por ello, aunque se necesite mucho tiempo, se logrará una unidad que sobrepase el actual localismo"[25] [The *Kaqchikel* dialect definitively constitutes an inescapable bulwark that supports other fields of action. Because of that, even though a lot of time will be required, it will gain a unity that will extend beyond (surpass) present-day colloquialisms].

Speaking and language define who we are. Bakhtin writes that "language invokes the political concept of freedom because it is the struggle against the necessity of certain forms" (Bakhtin 1981: 220). In order to project one's self into the non-indigenous world, learning to speak Spanish or English is an important step, but speaking the language does not guarantee access to the power or privilege inherent in the language for the native speaker. Language can be both an oppressor and a liberator because it does not serve all who use it equally. Bakhtin writes that "language is not a neutral medium that passes freely and easily into the private property of the speaker's intentions; it is populated, overpopulated with the intentions of others. Expropriating it, forcing it to submit to one's own intentions is a difficult and complicated process" (Bakhtin 1981: 294). He sees language as an interactive process, an interanimation. To be able to survive, both language and people must be able to exist in different layers of meaning and in different contexts, and must be able to understand both.

> As soon as a critical interanimation of languages began to occur in the consciousness of our peasant, as soon as it became clear that these were not only various different languages but even internally variegated languages, that ideological systems and approaches to the world that in no way could live in peace and quiet with one another—then the

necessity of actively choosing one's orientation among them began. (Bakhtin 1981: 296)

More than just understanding difference, and remaining outside and impartial, the process of self-fulfillment implies that one makes an ideological choice. However, it is possible to affect changes in one's self by mimicking the actions of others. In *Philosophy of the Act*, Bakhtin calls these people *pretenders*. If an individual sees the need to alter her behavior and yet does nothing, the process stops here, and the potential understanding is aborted. He writes:

> The abstract-sense aspect, when it is not correlated with inescapable actual uniqueness, has the character of a project: It is something like a rough draft of a possible actualization or an unsigned document that does not obligate anyone to do anything. Being that detached from the unique emotional-volitional center of answerability is a rough draft. . . . When we become ethically and cognitively answerable for our selves, we can rewrite [our] life once and for all in the form of a fair copy. (Bakhtin 1993: 54)

The production of the testimonial and the lifework of Víctor Montejo and Rigoberta Menchú is the literal projection of their *selves* and their words into the world at large.

Metamorphosis: The Conscious Volition to Change/Becoming the New Being

Metamorphosis represents a focal point from which self-determined change begins. It also represents the process of the change itself, often only seen from a point further along on the same axis, where one can look back and see that both outside and personal decisions have critically determined one's direction in life.

The decision to change, which emanates from inside a person in response to his understanding of the outside world and his effective power over it, constitutes actually learning to think differently about one's orientation with regard to the outside world. This process begins a metamorphosis that Paulo Freire calls *consciêntização* (becoming critically aware of one's life and surroundings). Bakhtin writes, "*Ought* becomes possible for the first time where there is an acknowledgment of the fact of a unique person's being *from within* that person, where this fact becomes a center of answerability, where I assume answerability for my own uniqueness, for my own being" (Bakhtin 1993: 51). This is the moment when metamorphosis occurs.

In his theory of novelistic development, Bakhtin sees metamorphosis from early times to the middle ages as a pre-novelistic element, which shows an individual from the viewpoint of crisis, "becoming other than what he was": a dramatic transformation, a man into an ass, a sinner into a saint. The focus is not evolutionary. This hagiographic triptych that characterized the life of the saints (i.e., sin, crisis and sainthood) has a contemporary counterpart, reconfigured in the authorship of the self. In self-authorship, metamorphosis hinges on the ability of the individual to come to terms with his own life—past, present and future—and take responsibility for it. The outcome of this process is a continually evolving transcendence, never completed because individuals continue to live actively. "The activity of my self-consciousness is always in effect and proceeds uninterruptedly through all lived experiences that are mine. Memory is for me the memory of the future" (Bakhtin 1990: 125).

For Rigoberta Menchú, this transcendence results in a shift from being defined and marginalized by others to being realized in herself. Her appropriation by Western culture is on her own terms, as herself, not only as *other*. She is a whole being whose reflection in the eyes of others yields more than just the image of her own self. This appropriation does not diminish, rather it enhances her image, culminating in Rigoberta Menchú's present and ultimate stature as *post-modern iconographic*, which I see as a model for transfiguration into secular sainthood.

Growth of a Self-Sustaining Person

The image of the emerging (wo)man begins to surmount her private nature, and enter into a completely new, spatial sphere of historical existence.

M.M. Bakhtin

The growth of the self-sustaining person is the process of being in two places at once, which means understanding the limits between *self* and *other*. Víctor Montejo and Rigoberta Menchú as individuals are *other* in both worlds. The very nature of the process of *autoidentificarse*, the thrust of the personal development of all the main characters in these narratives, creates a bridge between two worlds, the one from which the speaker came and that which he addresses. Circumstances and their decisions with regard to themselves may differ, but these actors have aligned themselves with their own culture and ethnic identity. Their *otherness* is their reality. They are *other* in terms of the West. They are *other* in their own environment, as we shall see in the discussion of the testimonial. They are *another other* developed through the process of authoring the *self*, enabling them to be both independent and interdependent.

How can we understand another person's life and culture? Although the idea of *excess of seeing* is critical for dialogical growth and interaction, it is necessary to look at how Bakhtin sees the self-fulfilled person operating in this same context. For this he uses the concept of *vzhivanie* (live-entering). *Vzhivanie* represents the concept that an individual can live into another person's life and reality, and understand it, while never giving up her own. In fact, her return to her self and reflection on the other allows her to see the other as he is, and to contribute to that other person's being. To do so, a well-developed sense of the self is necessary. With this sense of the self, we can avoid selfish motives and projections. *False charity* for Paulo Freire is giving to *another* ostensibly what he needs—in reality, what we want to think he needs—that which subtly oppresses him rather than giving him what he wants for himself, on his own terms.

As readers, by *living into the life* of Rigoberta Menchú we can become ambient in our understanding, and begin to see the world through her eyes as well as our own. Bystanders do not participate in the growth process, they are like voyeurs. Passive understanding, Bakhtin goes on to say, only reproduces what is already in existence. The creative understanding that arises from dialogic response enriches and produces a new and vitally productive level of understanding or personhood which goes far beyond simple outsideness or otherness.

For Montejo, Menchú and Bakhtin, theories are nebulous and meaningless if the belief system that they represent is not transformed into action. All three present a compelling and deeded perspective on praxis, on the idea of ethical responsibility and on the relation of self/other as independent/interdependent.

Projection of the Self/Word into the World at Large

The process of self-fulfillment and reconciliation is expressed or encased in the idea of *voice*, the ability to speak for/project one's self. *Voice* in this case asserts who is allowed to speak for whom, and under what conditions. The literature (production and dissemination of lifework) I am using in this paper is the tangible expression of this completed internal dialogue, and the process by which it was realized.

The privileging of Mayan narrators, who record their testimonies and the transcription of fables and epics from their oral tradition, constitutes the last part of this hermeneutical process. It begins the voyage of the *word* and the *self* into the world at large. Mayan anthropologists, like Víctor Montejo, are writing and publishing to counteract not only inaccuracies, but also the romanticized defense of indigenous identity, an insidious form of oppression that valorizes specific static/fictive aspects of a culture and does not allow for growth or change in time.[26] Because Mayan people are becoming anthropologists and linguists to work with their own people, we have a reconciliation of the subject (anthropology) with its former objects. This reconciliation represents an attempt to reclaim territory that has been appropriated and deformed by outside influences.

The process of self-fulfillment and reconciliation I will be describing is not merely a matter of asserting one's identity. It is a matter of having freedom to be who the individual is already; and freedom to visualize who one might best become, or as Seamus Dean has said, "to realize one's intrinsic essence in some tangible form."[27] It is the freedom enjoyed by others to determine their identity as they wish, not the fulfillment or reflection of someone else's projection. It is self-empowerment. Paulo Freire, in *The Pedagogy of the Oppressed,* equates this freedom with responsibility and action. "To claim that men are persons and as persons should be free, and yet to do nothing tangible to make this affirmation a reality is a farce."[28] The projection of the self into the world through action is therefore an imperative conclusion to self-authorship or self-fulfillment. Because it is so, it expresses an ethical sense and a strong moral force, which relates not so much to the law and religion as it does to personal responsibility and integrity, as an integral part of the operative self. Bakhtin says that a philosophy of life can only be a moral philosophy and that the conception is of no value without an object through which it can be revealed or tangibly expressed. Therefore the real world is not the world as thought but as experienced (Bakhtin 1993: 122-24).

Rigoberta Menchú and Víctor Montejo present a compelling and deeded perspective on the idea of ethical responsibility. It is through the process of self-fulfillment that these two writers are able to articulate their philosophy and concretize it through action. Bakhtin further argues that any aesthetic act requires an act of love (a selfless concentration of time and energy), and it is that act of love which provides its driving force and impetus. Therefore, it is both ethics and love that bind an individual to praxis. Bakhtin observes pragmatically that a response of selfless love is not possible in every context, because it would be impossible to function in the world. About the path she has chosen Rigoberta Menchú writes:

> This is my cause. As I have already said, it wasn't born out of something good, it was born out of wretchedness and bitterness. It has been radicalized by the poverty in which my people live. It has been radicalized by the malnutrition which I, as an *Indian*, have seen and experienced, and by the exploitation and discrimination which I have felt in the flesh. And by the oppression that prevents us performing our ceremonies, and shows no respect for our way of life. At the same time they have killed those closest to me. Therefore, my commitment to the struggle knows no boundaries or limits. (Menchú 1984: 247)

Me llamo Rigoberta Menchú and *Testimony: Death in a Guatemalan Village* express a willingness to die for one's beliefs. Xuan, the hero of *El Kanil*, has to give his life to save his people. Rigoberta Menchú loses most of her family through kidnapping, torture and murder. Her father is burned alive in a political action in the Spanish Embassy. At the time of the transcription of *El Kanil*, Víctor Montejo's brother is *disappeared*. His testimonial concerns the mass murders by the military in the village where he is a school teacher, and by his own near death experience. What are we given to understand here with regard to the nature of self-fulfillment? What prompts the desire for reconciliation and self-fulfillment if the result of such consciousness leads to death, expulsion or canonization?

These narratives represent a perspective that only flowers by being in the world and doing. Bakhtin writes in *The Author and Hero* that the experiences of life are not part of epistemology and philosophy. A new vocabulary is needed, transcendent of genre, not just *more inclusive*, that does not sacrifice the quality of expression inherent in individual difference, and goes beyond institutional definitions of literature and values these narratives as discourses demonstrating social interaction and praxis. Bakhtin writes, "After all, the boundaries between fiction and non-fiction, between literature and non-literature, and so forth are not laid up in heaven." The idea that truth is universal is the "unfortunate legacy of rationalism" (Bakhtin 1981: 33). There are many differences to be resolved. Rigoberta Menchú reflects on her experience, and I quote her in extenso:

> There is something else we are discovering in Guatemala to do with intellectuals and illiterate people. We've learned that we haven't all got the ability of an intellectual. An intellectual is perhaps quicker and able to make finer syntheses. But nevertheless, others of us have perhaps the same ability for other things. Before, everyone used to think that a leader had to be someone who knew how to read, write and prepare documents, and our leaders fell into that trap for a time, and said, "I'll lead and you fight."
>
> At one time many of our leaders would come from the capital to see us in the *finca* (farm) and say, "You peasants are stupid, you don't read or study."
>
> And the peasants told them, "You can go to hell with your books. We know that you don't make a revolution with books, you make it through struggle." A leader must be someone who's had practical experience. It's not so much that the hungrier you've been, the purer your ideas must be, but you can only have a real consciousness if you have really lived this life. (Menchú 1984: 223)

Since it is not possible to experience *being* within the confines of the theoretical, to grow we must be prepared to relinquish unquestioned personal values and ideologies. First, theories must be wrested from isolation and integrated into life work and events. Then, theories can be developed through our observation about the nature of things. This is the hermeneutical process I see in these texts. In *Speech Genres and Other Essays*, Bakhtin writes that individuals should "avoid the false tendency toward reducing everything to a single consciousness, toward dissolving it in the other's consciousness" (Bakhtin 1986: 141). All three of these writers have an active individualism that presents a prospect for true trans-culturality. I believe that Montejo and Menchú have become, respectively, *another other* who can operate fully in both worlds; they are cultural mediators who do not lose track of origins. They represent a special type of solidarity, rather than the sameness that is the result of the practice of *theorism*.

Intertext:

The Behavior of Discourse in a Contradictory World

Amid the good things of this here and now world are also to be found false connections that distort the authentic nature of things, false associations established and reinforced by tradition and sanctioned by religious and official ideology. Objects and ideas are united by false hierarchical relationships inimical to their nature. These false links are incorporated by scholastic thought and by a false theological casuistry shot through with centuries of error. It is necessary to destroy and rebuild this false picture of the world. It is necessary to liberate these objects and permit them to enter into the free unions that are organic to them *no matter how monstrous these unions might seem.* On the basis of this new matrix of objects, a new picture of the world necessarily opens up a world permeated with an internal and authentic necessity.

M.M. Bakhtin, *The Dialogic Imagination*

The words that frame this section of text were written by Bakhtin while in exile, culminating his exhaustive, recondite, even Talmudic study of the Western intellectual tradition. Although the purpose of this text is specifically to show the parallel discourse of Bakhtin and Menchú on the idea of the *articulated self,* words and ideas do not exist in isolation, but are read in the contemporary context of the post-modern, post-colonial era that Bakhtin has called *the here and now world* (Bakhtin 1981: 169). Furthermore, we as readers *live into* a text. In other words we enter into the life of the story as a participant: animated or bored, understanding the interaction or lost in a conversation that seems foreign to us. This engagement is never unidirectional. We and the text are changed.

On another level each one of us as individuals represents a text in the sense that life is written on the body and all the variables that are assumed in a text are assumed in our lives. There are two exceptions: our birth and conception, a part of another's history; and our death, experienced by those who do not die. We read others' actions; we edit our life stories by forgetting and changing our minds, as well as when we mature in our thinking. We publish as we speak and often, our narratives are ambivalent or equivocal. Always, we bear in and on our bodies the lifework of our experience.

The struggle to reconcile the world as reported by others and the world as personally experienced has been dynamically reflected in the life work of artists of color throughout the twentieth century. This parallels the discrepancy that often exists between life and theory. Literature/writing as lifework has provided a previously unresolved venue of expression. The "novel" has become a sentient, non-linear history and testimonial of life events, not only a tool for colonial discourse. In the West, the Nobel Prize in Literature has focused our attention on how marginalized people have affected discourses on dominant ideas about the nature of literature. Its sister, the Nobel Peace Prize, focused attention on Rigoberta Menchú's attitude toward her own oppression.

Bearing these things in mind, a segue is necessary to discuss some issues that impinge on the interpretation of texts in contemporary scholarship and subsequently, how they have affected the reception and interpretation of Rigoberta Menchú's text. I would like to encapsulate them here, because although they need to be discussed, I do not wish them to bleed over into the body of the text diluting the potency of the textual comparison that follows.

Bakhtin's Idea of the Western Intellectual Tradition

Historically, especially through interpretations of science and religion that coalesced during the enlightenment, the dominant mode of thought in the West has demonstrated a proclivity to impress external form on things that already have inherent and valuable forms of their own. Modernism manifested itself in the belief in a universal referent, ultimate homogeneity and hierarchical structures. It showed how, through science, the "polarization into man: nature, the means to man's self-consciousness, was exaggerated by the scientific revolution into an exclusive disjunction."[29] These days, in the post-modern Western world, a lack of universal referent often signals degeneration of form, upending traditional ideas of authority. For others, however, this universal referent never existed or if it did, it did so only in the negative, or without reference to Western hegemony.[30]

Bakhtin counters perceived ideas of uniform hierarchical structures (either a model with a uniform/arbitrary center and margins or a sequential/genealogical model, each with their fables of legitimization) with an interactive one based on difference. Bakhtin's model investigates and integrates material that was minimized and often ignored by dominant discourses, but was still vital to an adequate interpretation of the Western tradition. These two views of the Western tradition are at odds. One, although enlightening, leaves us subjects of external discursive practices impressed by outside sources, while the other abjures sameness. His world is not a world off-center or entropic, but rather a world in which a uniform center does not or did not ever exist. For this reason it is useful for comparisons of cultural production. Bakhtin's analysis of the Western intellectual tradition is unique because he uses it to show how language and meaning (ideology) are deeply related although they can only be interpreted in an individual context, an *utterance*. The basic structural units are the individual and the word, and they detail as well as parallel each other. Every individual inhabits a unique world framed by his consciousness. Our judgments are made using subjective beliefs and ideas about assumed values and behaviors. These assumed values and behaviors are what give hegemony its potency. Yet, each person has a different set of ideas and environments that she brings to the words she speaks. Not only do our cohorts affect us, our ways of addressing the world and our speaking styles place us within certain cultural frameworks for outsiders. Our perceptions inform our actions; consequently, our self-consciousness leads to social consciousness.

Because his unit of comparison is the individual and the word, Bakhtin now meets the post-modern world at the juncture of its feeling of fragmentation and loss of purpose. Using the commonality of Western intellectual history, he offers an innovative reinterpretation: This post-modern, post-Marxist, post-colonial world is a modal interregnum, a necessary realignment. Our selves, words and meanings enter this contradictory world filled with the expectations of the speakers and the listeners, with differing intellectual and cultural baggage. "Questions connected with those aspects in the life of discourse that have had not light cast on them by linguistic and stylistic thought . . . must deal with the life and behavior of discourse in a contradictory and multi-languaged world" (Bakhtin 1981: 275). An individual's paradigm (portfolio) of reference will determine what material will be looked for, discussed and interpreted. So, what is at question in this segment is the effect of perceived reality on discourse.

Naming and Heteroglossia

The process of naming involves designating meaning and assigning value. These strategies, enforced by coercive and non-coercive power, result in the denial of the integrity of the form or individual, or the violation of it. In its most physical or concrete form this type of objectification, turning a *subject* into an *object*, constitutes rape. The Western gaze has bared the spirit and later decried its nakedness.[31]

In assessing the onomastic fantasy of modernism, Bakhtin concedes that at one point there was the possibility—*the mythical Adam*—of naming, then heteroglossia took over and it was never possible thereafter (Bakhtin 1981: 278). Heteroglossia[32] fights against the ideological norm that has been imposed on language by dominant influences. Heteroglossia molds and changes words unintimidated by assumed meaning. This is how we enter the world of wandering and promiscuous signifiers, so aptly identified by Antonio Benítez Rojo in *The Repeating Island*. In Bakhtin's model there is no quiet on the Western Front.

Even as Bakhtin discusses the appropriation of discourse (and the apportionment or assignment of meaning) using the "authoritative and sanctified word of God" as an example, he writes, "[H]ere is the whole spectrum of (possible) meanings—from an inert quotation to the most ambiguous, disrespectful view, which could be seen in a travesty or parody—sacrilege or piety" (Bakhtin 1981: 71-72). "Oh, My God!" can mean a wide variety of things. With the ineffability of the postmodern, the same words can provoke many different effects. The finite word is the origin of infinite units of meaning and each utterance is created and must be understood in its own context. If there were uniform meaning no one would need language.

> The word, directed toward its object, enters a dialogically agitated and tension-filled environment of alien words, value judgments and accents, weaves in and out of complex interrelationships, merges with some, recoils from others, intersects with yet a third group: and all this may crucially shape discourse, may leave a trace in all its semantic layers, may complicate its expression. (Bakhtin 1981: 277)

Words are charged with the intent of the speaker, and the intent of both the observer/listener and the originator/speaker is up for severe scrutiny. In life, as in textual analysis, both the observer/listener and speaker/originator are implicated in the phenomenon observed, not set apart.

> For the writer (of artistic prose) on the contrary the object revels first of all precisely the socially heteroglot multiplicity of its names, definitions and value judgements. Instead the virginal fullness and inexhaustibility of the object itself, a prose writer confronts a multitude of routes, roads and paths that have been laid down in the object by social consciousness. (Bakhtin 1981: 278)

Because the investigation and interpretation of both the writers intention and the text are subject to heteroglossia, we need to investigate our own assumptions as well.

Self-Consciousness

Bakhtin writes that an appropriate self-consciousness is missing, and it is self-consciousness that leads to social consciousness. A void within means a void without—nihilism. In short, we relinquish our imagination when we relinquished our belief in possibility. We cannot contend in an infinitely variable context, our post-modern world, because we started from outside assumptions and imposed form, rather than let the form respond to the object. In the world of late capitalism, where everything is commodified, things and objects endeavor to tell us who we are. The external continues to define the internal, trappings indicate intrinsic value.

Nevertheless, we must ask, "How, if the variety of meanings and therefore interpretations is infinite, can we begin to understand what is meant and how it is to be understood?" We begin by understanding our selves and our intentions with regard to a word or an individual, for they are the units that construct the world. The largest portfolio of understandings is our own, or can be, if we are reflective. No one has more undiluted experience than we have with ourselves. Memory provides transcripts that show just how imprecise our observations were, how definitely inconclusive. The corrective inquiry of this last century—including psychiatry (which assumes a universal psychology within certain limits) and post-colonial discourse (a defining of agency by former objectified subjects)—is a means to integrate sound and pictures that are now submerged as feelings, rather than as meaning; to understand "not what we feel, but where we are invested."[33] When Bakhtin wrote, "Memory for me is the memory of the future," he was not speaking clairvoyantly. His statement was hermeneutical in the manner of retroactive anticipation, a personal fable of legitimization. "We do not have memories *of* childhood, but memories *on* our childhood, which do not arise out of the past, but are formed *sur le tard* (later on)."[34] Inasmuch as an exact replica of anything is impossible, we can say that memory is fickle, not necessarily capricious, a composite influenced by immediate surroundings and anticipations about the future. Memory cannot exist without time any more than chronology can exist without agency. Bakhtin is adamant that this transcendent sense of self-consciousness produced by living in uncertainty will open us to the possibility of understanding ourselves and necessarily others through his special application of praxis, which he calls *life entering* (Bakhtin 1993).

Let us return to some ideas from the first section of this text: Early autobiography was the beginning of the definition of the individual in a new age, and therefore parallels our own redefinition in the *here and now world*. Bakhtin reminds us that the Greeks saw both the first autobiography and, in conjunction with it, the breakdown of the unified image of the person in the form of the externally self-defined individual. He writes that any new age undergoes a transformation of the idea of identity and that this identity is tied to the new age, carrying with it the traces of the old—a different and unique sense of history that must be worked out. Utopian ideals need not become stylized nostalgic retrospectives anymore than the demise of the ideal of universal truth means that there is no truth and nothing to relate to. In the *here and now world* we are actually interactive. Each of us is unique, not alone.

> [T]he task of assuming a complete personality is conceived [in Rabelais] as the growth of a new man combined with the growth of a new historical era, in a world that knows a new history but that is also connected with the death of the old man and the old world. (Bakhtin 1981: 240)

Our dilemma is this: What we thought we knew is not in keeping with what we can see if we look around. Our understanding will be different one year from now and there is no longer any predictability to offer external control. Bakhtin, Menchú and academics of whatever portfolio look at the same phenomenon and can with that phenomenon destroy or build. We cannot truly be concerned about our influence on others if our discursive practice is based in destruction or if it ignores the context of the text as it was written, any more than we can have a philosophy that sustains itself without an ethical system to engage it.

Still, hope comes from the same story as nihilism. In a way, nihilism's affirmation of itself is identical with the will to overcome or its reversal, turning back onto itself.[35] Because there is affirmation, there is possibility, and because there is possibility, there can be hope. The transcendent nature of hope, however, is not disturbed by temporal events. Focusing on the problem today as if it would remain constant is not a satisfactory solution; we are prolonging the discussion that has been so deleterious to all of us. Dismantling the system will perhaps help us see what went wrong but it will not give us a new viable model. Bakhtin, I believe, describes a condition that is positively postmodern.

Bakhtin's Relationship to Foucault's Theories

There are externally based configurations related to the control of meaning that influence us and to which we can refer. Foucault made his life work tracing hegemony and the exercise of power in the West that makes or endeavors to make us subjects. There are things that we can take from him and his work will remain pivotal until we can address adequately the questions and examples that he raises/invokes. Often the space, opened through coercive force or hegemony, allows for contemplation and reassessment of outside influences. This is the case with Menchú and Montejo. The power of hegemony lies in our acquiescence to it. Its power is mediated by applied personal responsibility, and hope that enables us to look forward.

The first thing with which to deal is the recognition of the structure and nature of coercive and non-coercive power relations, as they have manifested themselves in the discourse of the West. (Foucault, through Nietzsche, offers a general genealogy of knowledge to date.) The power of Foucault was that he provided for the West an etiology or archaeology that brings us to the single footstep behind which we now stand. He showed how discursive practices, not merely theories, affect us. In this we are changed forever. Foucault himself became untiringly active in social issues especially in the riots of 1968. Using his fame to call press conferences on behalf of others who would not otherwise have been heard, he provided a space where others could speak for themselves.

Baudrillard may be correct when he says that Foucault carefully fills all the boxes he provides us for the trip out from subjectification, *à huis clos* (behind closed doors). Foucault's work is a spreadsheet with accounts resolved, but the pervasive hopelessness leaves me divorced from my sensibilities. I could see myself as only a victim. We may and must begin from where we stand and define our positions in much the same way as we locate ourselves on a map. We understand that although this marks place, those things that we bring with us make up the lens with which we detail what we see, our *gaze*, our memory of the future.

In Bakhtin's idea of things, I no longer need to look over my shoulder, to view my past as if it were a specter. The past is in the wrong direction. Besides, the trip to the origins of things is dizzying and inconclusive. *Why* leads to closure and absolutes. I do need to understand *how* I came to be in this space in order to survey the terrain of my *here and now world*. Benítez Rojo writes, "[B]ut here we are not interested in trips to the origins of things, for no matter how pleasant they may be they usually lead to the vertigo that comes with a desire to explain what can't be explained" (Benítez Rojo 1994: 77). Although a forward gaze allows me to hope, without this consciousness being in the present is no guarantee of resolution, transformation, or movement. Nevertheless, the way out is through, not back. Foucault's structure attenuates itself as it moves from coercive to non-coercive, through dividing practices and subjectification, to the possibility of being the subject of one's own discourse.

At this point, we have another tool to inventory the traces. Antonio Gramsci tells us in his *Prison Notebooks* that the past has left in us the intent and meaning behind the words we speak. He defines language as:

> A totality of determined notions and concepts and not simply and solely of words grammatically void of content. Every level of language or utterance is permeated with definite concepts of the world; in every person one finds a bundle of contradictory notions, what is called "common sense" notions imposed mechanically by certain social groups.[36]

Foucault, having showed us the ways in which we have absorbed external opinion, gives way to Gramsci and reassessment. In Gramsci we see not only cultural traces but personal choices. Using as a model what Gramsci saw as a life inventory, the starting point for a critical elaboration of consciousness, for myself, begins from the place where I now am, at the locus of possibility, the *here and now world* where I spend my time. If Foucault does not succeed in being other than what he critiques, because he writes within the confines of certain processes of the West and is bound by them, Bakhtin visualizes a different way of seeing, and this vision relieves us of a specified sequential process, offering the models of chronotope and heteroglossia as well as the charged environment of interanimated meaning and living, whose beginnings he traces from other Western sources. Without the work of Foucault, corroborating and assessing the forces of externally imposed power, Bakhtin's ideas might have appeared more dreams than discourses of liberation. Menchú also describes a different order within her text. The result of this assessment is the progress of self-authorship, as discussed in this book, that allows us to displace ourselves and see another.

Author/Editor/Truth

The issue of authorial function is often fodder for academic debate in the context of the testimonial. Was there an author of this book, if there is no autonomous self and we are all products of discursive practices? If so, who? De Bray or Menchú? Ironically, Bakhtin has had several books attributed to him that he may not have written.[38] Benítez Rojo writes:

> Another of post-modern literary criticism's concerns lies in demystifying the concept of the author, and erasing the *creator aura* with which modern criticism endows him. For the post-structuralist critic, looking at the literary task from the post-modern standpoint, the author, far from being a creator of worlds, is a technician or artisan whose job is controlled by a pre-existing practice or discourse. (Benítez Rojo 1993: 153-54)

Who wrote Menchú's text should be more of concern to Menchú than to either academics and critics. It is her life about which she was speaking, notwithstanding the effect that outside circumstances had on her lifework. Remember, Menchú could not read Spanish, and was only just learning to speak when she dictated the text over fifteen years ago. Now, she can read and write Spanish, she understands some English and has written several poems and another text in Spanish. If she had fault to find with the presentation or editing of the first book, *Me llamo Rigoberta Menchú*, she surely could have created a second edition, as we all might do given the funds and the power at her disposal. At the very least she might have written a disclaimer, something that has not been forthcoming. She has chosen to write *El Clamor de la Tierra*, detailing more about the peasant movement and the events that influenced its ten-year development to the date of publication, 1992. This text locates Menchú outside of the world of the *paisano,* in the network of the international struggle for resistance and the world of the CUC within the hegemony of *Ladino*/Mayan cooperation. She calls this phase of her struggle *un nuevo amanecer* (a new dawn).

Bakhtin has a non-proprietary attitude toward authorship because of the innumerable influences that accountability, dialogism and culture place on the word. That is not to say that one is not responsible for one's text/self in the world. The ownership of the act is an unavoidable responsibility. So, we could say that in its generative aspect we are participants under the influence and we are co-authors with regard to interpretation. Bakhtin's comments are to the point:

> [T]he image of the author—if we are to understand by that the author-creator—is a contradiction in terms; every image is created, and not a creating, thing. And this image of the author cannot, of course,

enter into the fabric of images that makes up the literary work. However if this image is deep and truthful, it can help the listener or reader more correctly and profoundly to understand the given work of an author. (Bakhtin 1981: 257)

An editor can change a text; my text or hers is no exception. The issue is who, if anyone, maintains control over the discourse presented. This is especially important in the testimonial. Menchú acknowledges a myriad of reflections as existing in her sense of self and others. Bakhtin wrote from exile that we all exist as tangents to any given discourse, at any place and time, but we can function ambiently on many levels and terrains. This is heteroglossia at work; modulating, not aimless. Both Menchú and Bakhtin understand the need to project the self and stay connected to the people. Primary reliance on individual process is a very Western, fairly recent concept.

To what is Menchú testifying? She is testifying to her individual perception and her personal experience, a sentient historicity, not a linear construction. This is not just her past and her present but the political and ideological upheaval that has been Guatemala's, the heroism of her father and her family, terrorism and its relationship to the development of the CUC, as well as the changes in her life, profoundly spiritual that allow her to grow.

We must avoid the false tendency toward reducing everything to a single consciousness, toward dissolving into another's consciousness (while being understood). . . . One cannot understand understanding as emotional empathy as the placement of the self in the other's position (loss of one's own position). One cannot understand understanding as a translation from the other's language into one's own language. (Bakhtin 1986: 141)

Life/Text/Culture

Bakhtin's word resonates in the world of the *other* because of his particular, dialogical view of intellectual tradition. Bakhtin writes that once an experience leaves the realm of a lived life it becomes an abstraction, culture. He shows how this results in a collective subject. Equally importantly, he shows that abstractions do not make people accountable. Abstractions allow people to objectify others, on all sides. We must return again and again to the individual and her process, the real life, not the abstractions that come from theorism (Bakhtin 1993). As Freire recently wrote, "Respect for popular knowledge then necessarily implies respect for cultural context. Educands' concrete localization is the point of departure for the knowledge they create of the world; 'their' world, in the last analysis, is the primary inescapable face of the world itself."[37] Bakhtin tells us that only an outsider can tell us certain things, not who we *are* but how we are perceived by the outside, as a part of our immediate context. He also writes:

> Characteristically it is not private life that is subjected to and interpreted in light of social and political events, but rather the other way around; social and political events gain meaning [in the novel] only thanks to their connection with private life. (Bakhtin 1981: 190)

Menchú positions herself at the first moment of her dialogue with us and her culture, in the opening lines of her story. There is no doubt about how she views her ideological, political and spiritual reality, which will be discussed later in this study. The process described in this text, corroborated in both Montejo and Bakhtin, has produced a woman with high political ideals and acumen, strong ideology and faith. Possessing limited understanding of the world outside Guatemala and no background in Western philosophy, Rigoberta Menchú used the tools at her disposal. Menchú has a very sophisticated, humane way of being in the world that could not be read fully with only a Western perspective. Menchú clearly filled a need in current theory that focused on the necessity to reunite theory with life. In fact, this is precisely why Rigoberta Menchú needs to be honored as speaking from her private life. Menchú's life work is proof of Bakhtin's argumentative structure. Yet, Menchú's words do not live in the West as she uttered them, rather they are configured, through heteroglossia, in the minds of Western theorists according to their own suppositions.

In English, we speak about the events of our lives being *written on the body*, of the *body as text* or *body language*. When any critic writes in the name of scholarship, rupturing to open up new ways of seeing, what happens to the life of the body in question, when body of text and body of individual are part and parcel of each other? How much more so when that text is the testimonial of an individual's life? This is also important for us as individuals as we pursue the conjunction of an integrated theory of being that reflects our lived lives.

What was an issue of criticism now becomes a precarious issue of ethics. I have a responsibility toward my text and the understanding of the words and life that I critique. Displacement is necessary for growth, but violence is not a prerequisite for understanding. Often critique, as *anti-conquest*, allows us to do violence to another's word/life with the same impunity as the *encomenderos* who came with the Conquest. If we look at the idea of self-consciousness, as I believe Bakhtin wrote about it, we will see that we are to scrutinize and reflect on our own words, as a continuing action in the present. We address a text not as an act of generosity but through a way of being, both reflective and benevolent. Because ideas in the postmodern *here and now world* are contiguous and changing; one act is not enough, any more than an act of contrition is equivalent to a change in consciousness, although both may occur at the same time. Resolution does not mean there is no tension, rather that we are responsible and keep things in appropriate focus. The extent of the problem we face is apparent when we acknowledge that war, whether as liberation or oppression, is a violent act in which people are killed. Liberation theology has its weakest moments when dealing with the issue of violence for the ends of peace.

For the Sake of Argument

An *argument* is a stylized way of leading someone into certain ways of thinking by presentation of a group of indicators. Until recently the definite lens through which the presenter was speaking was not necessarily given as preface to the discussion, because there were uniform assumptions about origins and directions. Since commonality is no longer assumed, *prima facie* interpretation is jeopardized.

Contentions about Menchú's text have arisen which coalesce around form and function vis-à-vis literature and critical process. These are institutional processes, not necessarily personal ones, but they affect individuals and need to be addressed, contextualized or displaced. For me, these do not consist of arguments against critique or scholarship, they reflect differences in ideologies and the disparity that exists in thinking between schools of thought in the academic world and their respective public postures. These contentions need closer scrutiny, in the light of the *lived life*.

With regard to *Me llamo Rigoberta Menchú*, the arguments are of two sorts: theoretical issues that do not apply to Menchú's world and endeavor to separate her from her self, and those that cast doubt upon Menchú's credibility. She exists as she says but the data she proposes are inaccurate, or false. The academic argument has been an objectifying argument that decontextualizes its subject. These arguments are sinister because they often push the limits of transgression, hoping not to be responsible thereafter. Often these arguments do not endeavor to decode the sign and see the specific meaning. One implication can be that Menchú, for example, does not understand her own reality. This *is* possible since we have seen or experienced this misunderstanding in ourselves, necessitating the descriptive shift from modern to post-modern theoretical structures. In *The Structure of Scientific Revolutions*, Thomas Kuhn describes exactly this circumstance as a *paradigm shift*. A paradigm shift occurs in scientific practice when observable phenomenon do not corroborate the theories generated to explain them. This results in the introduction of a new point of view with regard to the phenomenon that in turn causes great wakes of discarded intellectual detritus. This process, viewed from an inadequate perspective or a single focus, appears only as a mess, but it is in actuality the fallout resulting from a shift to a new theoretical framework. Although Kuhn was talking specifically about the world of science, there is a direct parallel between the construction of scientific and social theories. In fact, the development of theoretical concepts in both arenas often detail and delineate each other. Misunderstanding temporal reality does not negate personhood, but the assumption that an outside opinion about another is more valid than the individuals' sense of themselves and their understanding of their own reality annihilates. This is especially true when there is unmediated power involved.

Another aspect of academic discourse is the contestatory gesture, which disassembles the argumentative structure of another to prove a point. This is not critique. "Critique," Theresa Ebert writes, "points to what is suppressed by the empirically existing: what could be, instead of what actually is. Critique indicates in other words, that what *is* not necessarily the real/true but rather only the existing actuality that is transformable."[39]

Innocuous yet nevertheless belittling disparagement, in the context of argumentation, is academically okay, while paeans of hopefulness based on the same body of information are less so. This argumentation based in the idea of hierarchical structures is inimical to the *here and now world*. In a context of massive cultural genocide, my discomfort comes from its marginal productivity, except for the benefit it gives the writer. These texts remain within the production of the self, an insiders exclusionary commentary. There is no praxis. These discourses, published in periodicals and journals to which Menchú herself has no access, often transcend in academic circles the body and value of the text in hand.

Menchú rises from the other side with the malediction of intellectuals, going so far as to say, "The peasants say, 'You can go to hell with your books, you can only be a leader if you have lived this life'" (Menchú 1983: 223). She is upfront, and it is hard to accuse her of subterfuge.

In the culture of academia there is an unacknowledged anxiety when the underclasses successfully assert themselves outside the realm of popular mythology. Horatio Alger with his bootstraps is an exemplary model for all class-based behavior, outside the university. Lamentably, the *self-made man* in North America can endow a chair but cannot sit in it. Alger, the prototype, became canonized as an example of upward mobility in a transitional era of industrialization. But, he was satisfied with becoming middleclass. Underlying the ostensible content of this fable is the belief in improvement through education/schooling that runs against the grain of Menchú's *illiteracy*. Menchú shows us that you do not have to be a Western academic to do valuable intellectual work. Perhaps she touches a nerve as she describes what has always been part of her understanding of Mayan people: a unitary world view, a sense of history and the effective vision of the desire for a better life. Many in the West now perceive these phenomena missing in their own lives. Perhaps she sensitizes us to our own untested virtue.

Academic Theory and the Lived Life

To show how academic and personal discourses affect the text of the life of another, I will briefly address four academic texts, two deal specifically with the work of Menchú. The third is a strong theoretical piece, pivotal in contemporary post-colonial scholarship. The fourth is a work of a journalist anthropologist.[40]

As the testimonial of Menchú becomes more widely taught, the problem arises of how it is to be interpreted—as literature and therefore object, or as life. John Beverley, who has spent a substantial portion of his time writing and thinking about testimonial narrative writes first, in *Against Literature*, about his own portfolio of personal reference. This is a most valuable contribution to academic work. Because of his precedent, we as readers can understand what things have affected the context in which he reads and interprets, not only theory but lived life. In the chapter entitled "Ideology of the Literary" he writes, "As we have come to expect in densely constructed verbal objects of this sort, an indeterminacy of meaning arises between the explicit message of the [poem] and the rhetorical machinery put in motion to present it."[41] This describes exactly what happens to the testimonial in academia, even though Beverley limits his analysis to poetics. An act of displacement is necessary for growth, not of someone else, but of ourselves. This displacement allows individuals in the West to investigate our assumed virtue as well as the power inherent in going unnamed.

Menchú wrote to get out the word about what was happening to the Mayan people. Once the word is out there, an individual can exercise only a minimal amount of control over its interpretation. This makes for some problems. Menchú did not write for pleasure, so to look at the book in the traditional sense of literature is to misread from the outset. Nevertheless, reading the book in an academic setting can result in growth of understanding. Rigoberta Menchú is not the woman she was when that text was written. Her life has changed. Life through historical process also has intervened. The life of an individual grows and leaves the text behind. The text in its new context may leave the life behind. In a strange sense the text allowed her to become whom she already was. Appropriation and acceptance of course could pre-empt a long fought-for revolutionary function: having a voice and determining when and to whom to speak. Bakhtin writes in the context of his discussion of Rabelais, "The very attempt of the Renaissance to establish the Latin language in all its classical purity inevitably transformed it into a dead language" (Bakhtin 1981: 80).

Those who have been unable to speak, because of inadequate education, poverty or terrorism, can easily take a dim view of well-meaning academics. Very few academics born in the United States and Western Europe have experience with brutality, revolution or incarceration. These are out-class experiences, antithetical to the halls of ivy. This colors the academic discussion of texts like *My Name is Rigoberta Menchú*, and *Testimony: Death of a Guatemalan Village*. Nor are the underclasses engaged with academics, except through appropriation or in unusual circumstances. Interlopers are suspect on both sides. Once again it is isolation and lack of interanimation that cause us to atrophy.

Criticism of Rigoberta Menchú has also been focused on her refusal to divulge information, on her *secrets* as she puts it. Doris Sommer's "Rigoberta's Guarded Truth"[42] is problematic because of the way in which it questions Menchú's reserve. When we consider the context of her testimonial, written in the face of what she believed was the demise of her culture as she knew it, her own life as she might have wished it to be and her family as it was, under the most vile of circumstances, it would be hard to fault her for not telling everything. In this context, why would she tell all to a stranger? It is difficult to imagine that we ourselves would have done so under similar conditions. Even so, *My Name is Rigoberta Menchú* is in itself an act of trust.

Sommer's opening lines are, "It is surprising, I think, to come continually upon passages in Rigoberta Menchú's testimonial where she purposely withholds information—surprising because otherwise her denunciation of Guatemala's Indian removal policy seems so transparent." This introduction obscures the distinction between public and private practice inherent in Menchú's life/text. Menchú has bared her soul; "Rigoberta's Guarded Truth" decries its state of nakedness as inadequate. Sommer seems unwilling to concede to the life experience that has caused Rigoberta Menchú's reticence and projects coyness onto that reticence. By employing a trope of seduction and sexual innuendo to describe how Menchú presents her life/text to us, Sommer neutralizes Menchú's experience. She appropriates her vocabulary without the lived context, and in so doing, turns "No Secrets, Rigoberta's Guarded Truth" to her own textual advantage. The issue of the article then becomes not Menchú's lived life, but rather an occasion for comparative academic theory. This tactic is all the more egregious when one considers the fact that Menchú's narrative is a text dealing with rape. Two of the three texts Sommer uses in her critique are stories of literal rape, both personal and cultural.[43] Menchú understands the extent to which a seduction, when it is not mutual, turns a subject into an object. What Sommer sees as Menchú's attempt to *seduce* I read as a defiant cry for help from a woman who is desperately concerned about the abuse she has endured already and what has happened to the culture she loves. Having displaced herself with wary vulnerability, she has put herself out for us to read as part of the actualization of her consciousness.

Menchú's life is not part of the vulgarization and exploitation of tragedy—the stuff of television talk shows. In a culture where modesty and reticence are valued, such a personal testimonial recorded for strangers must seem profligate. It is not difficult to imagine that Menchú, who has her feet in two worlds as she narrates, has exceeded her cultural mores to publish her life experience.

Sommer refers to Nietzsche and states that his dilemma is worth mentioning in the context of Menchú's "textual strategy, to notice it and to respect its results" (Sommer 1991: 53). Yet, she continues to dwell on Menchú's reticence. Midway through Sommer's article we read, "That is why, at the end of a long narrative in which Rigoberta has told us so much, she reminds us that she has set limits which we must respect" (Sommer 1991: 60). We can see now that these alarming sexual innuendos are Sommer's textual strategy: bait to get us to read.

Investigating possible meanings for Menchú's *secrets*, Sommer offers plausible solutions on one hand and intimations of textual strategies on the other:

> My attention can be fixed on Rigoberta's secrets only because her refusal to tell remains on the page after editing is done . . . . They say in effect this document is a screen, in the double sense . . . something that shows and that too covers up. . . . Therefore the reader may wonder what "cannot know secrets" means and why so much attention is being called to our insufficiency as readers. (Sommer 1991: 53)

Sommer asserts that however we read it, we are "either intellectually or ethically unfit" for Rigoberta's *secrets* (Sommer 1991: 56). Menchú's political agenda is different from, although related to, the honor that she pays her culture, some of the sacred aspects of which she has refused to disclose to outsiders. She refrains because of cultural constraints and discretion. Sommer writes that there is "no presumption of immediacy between the narrating *I* and the readerly *you*, which she asserts has the political value of keeping us at a distance" (Sommer 1991: 52). She emphasizes that this testimonial is not a case of readerly text (*estar*) but of an explanation of Rigoberta Menchú's state of being (*ser*). As such, our personal deficiencies as readers have no relation to the text, except that our lethargy toward injustice is directly implicated in her story.

Rigoberta's secrets are political—what she has seen and done. They are also cultural and spiritual. Sommer notes that in every society there are many secrets that all its members understand.[44] She intimates that a degree of foreignness and cultural difference makes these secrets incomprehensible to the outsider. I concur, but I cannot assume that just being in Quiché longer will make *being Mayan* transparently comprehensible to me.

This is only part of Menchú's point. She has said enough, and she claims a right to privacy. Her lifework is going to people whom she can hardly imagine. Already, Menchú has said, and Sommer has quoted, that priests have come to Guatemala and missed the point of Mayan religious life. Those priests lived in Mayan communities, so on what basis should Rigoberta Menchú believe that a complete stranger would understand as much as she has said already, profoundly disturbing as it is? She cannot divulge her secrets because they rely on *sentimientos sin palabras* (feelings that cannot be expressed in words). "Personally," Sommer writes, "I prefer to think that her secrets are more literary than real. . . . Rigoberta's withholding . . . is a calculated investment in diversification" (Sommer 1991: 56-57).

In another interesting pairing of ideas, Sommer writes, "Rigoberta refuses to be redeemed from difference," and "our difference from that community is one of degree; maybe we are not so much outsiders as *marginals*, allies in a possible coalition rather than members. We are not excluded from her world but kept at arm's length" (Sommer 1991: 58-59). In my reading, we are both excluded from her world and kept at arm's length. We do not read the world the way Rigoberta Menchú does, because we are not and can never be what she exactly is: Maya Quiché. A polarity of excluded/included has to do with Menchú's idea of ethnicity, her point of origin. It is *difference* that has redeemed Rigoberta Menchú. There is no redemption in appropriation. The West is also kept at arm's length. Maya are rightfully skeptical of the insinuation of outsiders into their cultural practice. Coalition, which represents a third position outside of her sense of cultural practice and ethnicity, is supported by Menchú because of its potential for revolutionary action and personal growth.

Sommer continues, "For Rigoberta there are no ideal readers," pointing out that Quiché, those who Sommer feels could be ideal readers, cannot read (Sommer 1991: 61). Even though the Maya Quiché are interested in obtaining books written to elucidate their cultural practices, as we have read in the writings of Víctor Montejo, citizens of Europe and the United States are Menchú's *ideal* readers. Here are individuals who have both money and power to effect change, but who cannot or do not choose to imagine what most Maya already understand. Menchú's cultural experience with regard to her community is secondarily preserved. Sommer critiques Menchú's ideological practice by saying:

> [F]rom their marginal position vis-à-vis existing discourses, they may typically adopt features of several, not because they are unaware of the contradictions, but precisely because they understand that none of the codes implied by these categories is sufficient to their revolutionary situation. (Sommer 1991: 66)

While both we and they choose a variety of expressions for our ideology, since this is the prerogative of the post-modern conversation, the assumption that the Maya are "in a marginal position vis-à-vis existing discourses" implies that if it is not one of those recognized by the West, or chosen from Western practices, it has no merit. Maya do not necessarily wish to order their discursive strategies according to the precepts of the West. I see this borne out in the texts discussed in this study. A discourse of resistance and *autoidentificarse* is exemplified in Menchú's text.

Sommer clarifies her reading of Menchú's use of *we* and *I*, different in the testimonial than the autobiography:

> The phenomenon of a collective subject of the testimonial is, then, hardly the result of personal style on the part of the writer who testifies. It is a translation of a hegemonic autobiographical pose into a colonized language that does not equate identity with individuality. It is thus a reminder that life continues at the margins of Western discourse and continues to challenge it. (Sommer 1991: 59)

The phenomenon of the collective subject is cultural. The voice of Menchú in the testimonial is dialogic. It functions as her own and as a collective voice, which may be at once the same and different. In English the linguistic grain runs the opposite direction. English usurped and translated the collective subject into the hegemonic pose of royalty and gave it to the Queen, thereby creating a royal *we*. The collective subject, as the Maya experience it—if we can conceive it—is stillborn in translation.

Sommer points out ironically that Laclau and Mouffe, whose Marxism she critiques, have not considered the actual nature of the testimonial and who is writing it. This has resulted in "a reifying distance from the Latin American subject . . . which is more patronizing than respectful" (Sommer 1991: 68). She concludes:

> To read testimonials, curiously, is to mitigate the tension between first world self and third world other. I do not mean this as a license to deny the differences, but as a suggestion that the testimonial subject may be model for respectful, non-totalizing politics. There is no good reason for filling in the distance that testimonials safeguard through secrets with either veiled theoretical disdain or with uncritical hero-worship. Instead, that distance can be read as a lesson in the condition of possibility for coalitional politics. It is similar to learning that respects the condition of possibility for the kind of love that takes care not to simply appropriate its object. (Sommer 1991: 69)

The relationship between the voice of the life in question and the transcription of the text is a study in the ethics of cultural mediation. How can another's story, told in this case in the hermeneutical style of Mayan discourse, be converted or transported, if you will, into the sequential narration expectations of the English- and French-speaking population of Western Europe and the United States? At what price?

Trinh Minh Ha, in writing about cultural transcription in ethnographic writing, and in a sense about all translation, observes:

> The natural outcome of such a rationale is the arranged marriage between "experience distant" and "experience near" between the scientist's objectivity and nature's subjectivity, between insider's output and outsider's input. To get at the most intimate, hidden notions of the Other's self, the man has to rely on a form of neo-colonial interdependency.[45]

The work of Menchú must be judged by the depth and insight of its content. Although literary merit is an insider's question, Elisabeth Burgos De Bray has provided an excellent rendition of the oral text that contributed to the book receiving the Casa de Las Américas prize, which she, not Menchú, received. We cannot say that De Bray exerted no influence on the text. She had the power to produce this mediated text, she spoke a metropolitan language, and she was inclined toward ethnography by her training in anthropology. Her former husband was the revolutionary thinker, Regis De Bray.

Menchú did not remain behind in the naive world of the identified *other*, delineated by outside observation. In her *lived life*, she provides a concrete example of the text in hand: she is known to many of us, we have spent time with her, and we may recognize her patterns of speech and tone of voice. We can read her person as she speaks as text, whether she is on video, the national news or at a community meeting. The composite of her physical reality restores both the imagination and sentience, which might have been illusive in a single element; she never becomes an abstraction. The popular canonization of Menchú's book is based in its ability to reach beyond fact to produce depth of feeling and personal growth. Menchú is aware I believe of the limits of her text and is without pretensions about it. It is the mediated text of *another other*, another among others who has turned her experience into something that shares a commonality among those who are its subject and those who read it as well.

Menchú's text is not just a correction for leftist politics. Left and Right are the two sides of an ideological (binary) coin that will not spend in the new world market. The testimonial, *Me llamo Rigoberta Menchú*, mimics revolutionary action that increases visibility, corrodes power relations, and modifies behavior without limiting possibilities. As an ethical and articulated human being and icon: *post-modern iconographic*, flanked by her CNN bodyguards armed with video cams, Rigoberta Menchú functions in a semiotic capacity. Her present position as a post-modern icon serves Menchú as she serves and mediates for the thousands of others who (in living) participate in the process with somewhat less success.

Iconography and Subalterity

Gayatri Chakavorty Spivak, in her legendary article "Can a subaltern speak?", deconstructs the "ferocious standardizing benevolence"[46] of Western discourse whose disqualifying gaze has determined, constructed, essentialized and appropriated the *other*. Spivak argues that a subaltern cannot speak in the discourse of the West because her real voice gets lost or appropriated. "If in the context of colonial production the subaltern has no history and cannot speak, the subaltern as female is even more deeply in shadow" (Spivak 1988: 287). Spivak speaks in part from her own experience: as an Indian; a woman; and a complex intellectual in academia, once marginalized relative to the center of its discursive practices.

Who is subsumed under the protective discursive aegis "subaltern" and how can we recognize them? Subaltern seems to be almost synonymous with *other* even though Spivak states that the subaltern is "irretrievably heterogenous" (Spivak 1988: 284). Do subalterns recognize themselves as such outside of Western influence? *Subaltern* itself is an abstract category, that remains a theoretical being in Western discourse rather than a real person. "Individuals speak," Bakhtin writes, "through their *lived life*." In any case, when we name something, we develop a set of expectations based on the perceived meaning invested in that naming (subaltern), which are reinforced through hegemonic power relations.

The question, "Can the subaltern speak in Western discourse with its theoretical proofs and Marxist or capitalist agenda?" is different from my own prescriptive one: "Is it honorable to acknowledge this sometimes almost overwhelming difficulty and move to other ways of understanding?" The critical question becomes "Where and how can these new dialogic models be derived?" They depend on displacement, from individuals whether Western, marginalized or in exile. At its roots, the problem of who can speak or have a voice reflects the hearers value system, not necessarily an inherent lack of clarity or value in the other, although the idea often exists that it would be naive to believe anything else. Our anticipation of the event is what makes us attentive. Without a displacement of the privilege inherent in the West's vision of itself, the disclaimer that the subaltern cannot speak sets the stage for interpretation rather than honor of a different voice that may be incomprehensible to us. Negation of the other's ability and reiteration thereafter sets up a possibility for someone to become the arbiter of their power. In other words, to participate in any conversation about herself, the subject in question must exert undue energy countering the assumptions inherent in the given name. Bakhtin reminds us:

> Understanding is impossible without evaluation. The person who understands must not reject the possibility of changing or even abandoning his already prepared viewpoints and positions. In the act of understanding, a struggle occurs that results in mutual change and enrichment. (Bakhtin 1986: 142)

What I see in Menchú's text is the process by which a colonized individual, extruded through terror and coercion into the world of the West, proceeds to a unique and articulate sense of herself. Rigoberta Menchú does speak to us through her text even though it is blanketed by the agenda of her interlocutor, Burgos De Bray. It is her particular understanding of her life that draws us to her. Arturo Arias has referred to this phenomenon as the "numbing humility" of her narrative. Because I read her presence permeating *Me llamo Rigoberta Menchú*, I see evidence here that *subaltern* is neither a fixed identity nor a static category.

Spivak poignantly asks, "How can we touch the consciousness of the people even as we investigate their politics? With what voice-consciousness can the subaltern speak?" (Spivak 1988: 285). Do we speak through the mediated understanding of the needs and desires of those whom we represent (their theory of interests) or do we speak through ideology to represent preemptively those whom Western theory indicates are without a voice? Spivak writes that when womens' groups based in the West address women in *comprador* countries, they must understand that to "confront them is not to represent them but to learn to represent ourselves," and "the post-colonial intellectuals learn that their privilege is their loss" (Spivak 1988: 295). Here Spivak resolves one problem of Western post-colonial thinkers, addressed in this text as the internalization and assessment of external opinion, but her alluring argument has done little to clarify the inherent value of those whom we cannot hear because we have set about to explain ourselves. It does not seem to move from the dialectic to the dialogic. "In seeking to learn to speak to (rather than listen to or speak for) the historically muted subject of the subaltern woman, the post-colonial intellectual systematically *unlearns* female privilege," and a bit further on, "[T]his systematic unlearning involves learning to critique post-colonial discourse with the best tools it can provide not just simply substituting the lost figure of the colonized" (Spivak 1988: 295). Bakhtin writes that one must "come to feel at home in the world of other people in order to be able to go from confession to objective aesthetic contemplation, from questions about meaning and searchings for meaning to the world as a beautiful given (Bakhtin 1991: 11).

Even if "representation has not withered away," as Spivak writes, in the light of what Bakhtin envisioned, we can mediate on behalf of others. The question is the projection of individual meaning into the world and how that action is perceived and accomplished. We must honor and endeavor to understand the conceptual world of those who either wish to speak to us or with whom we wish to communicate. This is how Bakhtin's dialogism and *live entering* are applied in the post-colonial world. The process of dialogic assessment, delineated in this study, is not limited to the non-Western world. One of them can be one of us, for none of us is unaffected, even though we may be working with a different palate of oppressions, more subtle in the West, but no less convincing. Not all of us are brave enough to speak, even when we can, and I think this is the salient point of Montejo's *Death of a Guatemalan Village.*

Without this displacement of ourselves there is neither resolution nor praxis. The potentially interactive, dialogic situation stalls at the juncture between what Bakhtin calls *theorism* (the application of abstractions) and *pure empathy* (the cloying identification with another's oppression). This empathy is nothing more than the impression of our ideas onto the lives of others, which suppresses the heteroglossia of words and the dialogism that is inherent in human interaction.

The Maya do speak, but in Guatemala terrorism and poverty have both demeaned and minimalized their conversation. Maya are working to decide what they have to say to us and what they need from us, whether it be goods or protection, as they as a nation move from feudal interaction into their own agency in the contemporary world. For me, the idea of the subaltern does not exhaust human possibilities. People in poverty theorize about the immediate just as those with privilege deal with their immediate needs first. It is necessary be aware of one's situation to postulate an alternative and to prepare a defense against it.

I want to refer here to Spivak's discussion of the oppression of women and how this oppression, in the context of Montejo's *Death of a Guatemalan Village*, allows the women to interact and react because they have been ignored and culturally objectified. Even existing visibly, they have been *disappeared*. Transparent as they are to the military, they are visible and engaged in the rescue of the village. The men are in the thralls of a material manifestation of coercive power, the military and its weapons.

Spivak moves at the end of her paper into a discussion of Pierre Macherey and his interpretation of ideology. The discussion is reminiscent of the problem Sommer had with Menchú remaining silent about her *secrets*. Also, it addresses the nature of the silence, which belongs to the oppressed and unarticulated, about whom Montejo writes in *Testimony: Death of a Guatemalan Village*. Macherey's insight and Spivak's quote tie the problem together with clarity:

> What is important in a work is what it does not say. This is not the same as the careless notation "what it refuses to say," although that would in itself be interesting: a method might be built on it, with the task of measuring silences, whether acknowledged or unacknowledged. But what this work cannot say is important, because the elaboration of the utterance is carried out, in a sort of journey to silence. (Spivak 1988: 286)

The colonization of caste-based India and the Maya in Guatemala have been quite different. Guatemala is not yet a place of teeming metropolitan/factory life. Maya are rural people who negotiate the urban and *hacienda/finca* lifestyles. The rise of *maquiladora* production will certainly affect the application of a Marxist model, especially along the borders of the Usumacinta River where many refugee camps are located. This labor pool is triply displaced, making its way in exile. Left to their own process they may well develop a more dialogic model.

Each theory has its own blindfolds, but this neither forestalls nor dilutes the energy behind material goods and production, where Spivak draws her observations. Nevertheless, assumptions based in only material indicators limit possibilities and solutions. Although Spivak indicates through an argument, complex and rigorous, that the mode of material production is not the only measure of value, there is no element of the transcendent sense of things that opens up other ways to see outside the material/secular world. It is in the sentient world that the identification of the soul/spirit and its subsequent consciousness begin to develop their mediating strength. Consciousness is not a *deus ex machina* occurring outside the realm of the individual herself. Referring back to one of Gramsci's statements about consciousness:

> The fact is that only by degrees, one stage at a time, has humanity acquired consciousness of its own value and won for itself the right to throw off the patterns of organization imposed upon it by minorities at a previous period in history. And this consciousness was formed not under the brutal goad of physiological necessity, but as a result of intelligent reflection, at first by just a few people and later by a whole class, on why certain conditions exist and how best to convert the facts of vassalage into the signals of rebellion and social reconstruction.[47]

Spivak writes, in *Scattered Speculations on the Question of Value*, that "consciousness is not thought but rather the subject's irreducible intendedness toward the object" (Spivak 1988: 309). I understand that this object is not necessarily material. The development or adaptation of language systems to articulate necessary concepts follows. Language and people are not either primitive or not, or subaltern or not. Both always express that which needs to be expressed, to the level of understanding and perhaps a bit beyond if the imagination is intact. There are other language systems or cultural signifiers such as music, mime, painting, art of all types, gesture, kinship systems and dress. Theory is always contextualized. There are helicopters woven into *huipiles*, bombs woven into prayer mats, and the Diaspora itself that forces Mayans into the United States. When we see this lifework, we can see the articulation of opinion and resistance, people making and assessing their own history in the language medium in which they work best.

Expression, articulated as a word, an idea or an individual, becomes culture when it leaves the individual's personal sense of being, the *lived life*. Menchú describes the process by which her cultural identity becomes a personal, individual identity that remains interdependent with the world around it. Because of this, it is possible for Rigoberta Menchú to speak for her culture as a collective subject and yet not define the personal identity of others.

Menchú, encased in the Noble Prize, has been interpolated, providing a lexicon for us, delineating the collective aspects of the Mayan people. This lexicon can be used as a partial tool to help us see why the Maya speak, what they are saying and how they define their selves. As we move toward an understanding of the ubiquitousness of textuality and incessant change, flying as it does in the face of what was previously deemed permanence, the next issue is not the eternal one of "Who gets to speak?" but "What form will the text take?"

Interpreting Ideological Wars

An investigation of other Western texts that concern Mayan reality, written by anthropologists and other non-Mayan scholars, indicates a wide breach in the diversity of perception, both the conception of identity and the problems faced by Mayans, as well as how Mayans perceive themselves. While North American ideas about being Maya are enhanced by our vision about how things are or are meant to become, Bakhtin writes that *outsideness* can be a most powerful factor in understanding another culture. "It is only in the eyes of another culture that foreign culture reveals itself fully and profoundly. . . . Meanings engage in dialogue. . . . We raise new meanings for a foreign culture that it did not raise itself." Bakhtin writes that a living culture (or the word) emerges and evolves along with the world itself and reflects the historical emergence of the world. (Bakhtin 1986: 7)

David Stoll, a Stanford-trained anthropologist and journalist, has written extensively about the Ixil triangle of Quiché, raising some important questions about social analysis. Stoll has an impressive accumulation of data as well as a personal, journalistic confidence in his ability to get to the bottom of a problem in which, he acknowledges, he functions only as an outside observer. My concern is the interpretation of his data, the assumptions that his interpretations make. He seems particularly unaware of the nature of contemporary discourses outside anthropology that might affect his work and his self-reflection on his relation to it. Stoll's words have had an effect on discourses on Guatemala both within and outside the country, and have fueled great debate. But what actually is his narrative identity? Late in his book, *Between Two Armies in the Ixil Towns of Guatemala*, Stoll acknowledges his philosophical position by posing a critical problem:

> Once a population has been ravaged by war, what prevails is the hunger
> for stability, even on blatantly unfavorable terms. This puts scholars
> like myself who identify with the Left in an uncomfortable position.
> If subordinate groups usually do not want to pay the cost of defying
> dominant ones, where do we find a revolutionary subject to support in
> our work?[48]

In a Bakhtinian analysis we, as individuals, become the revolutionary subjects. The self-consciousness, which Bakhtin demands that we engage, begins and works itself out through the process investigated in the next two chapters of this study. It moves sometimes awkwardly through infinite units of complexity in theory, everyday life and group policy. Goals can be set, and these goals must be based in ethical considerations as well as in a sense of entitlements, which also need to be assessed in the light of power relations. In a Bakhtinian world where synthesis is seen as a monologic solution, the process of tolerance is a means and not an end in any case. So, Stoll's assumption is on very slippery ideological terrain. Our solutions do not always play out with similar ends in the rest of the world. Solutions must arise from and honor the people who share the problem. It is imperative to accept that there are as many interpretations of the world in Ixil as there are here, even when they are contradictory and even when we might believe that these visions of the world are inadequately informed. As Víctor Montejo said to me quietly one day, "There are millions of Maya and we are all thinking."[49]

Are the Ixil meant to be more interested in revolution because they are perceived by outsiders to be oppressed, and because revolution is the solution for oppression? Revolution is an abstract concept, hunger is not. Inasmuch as we can only interview willing survivors, and thousands of the folk involved were killed, disappeared, in exile, living in fear or only in the memory of the past, our data are skewed. The dead could tell other stories. How does Stoll read silence, rivalry and ambivalence? What is the agenda of those to whom he is speaking, and what is their relation to power? He inadequately discusses his understanding of the difference between response to a direct question in an interview, information offered in casual conversation in another context and that knowledge with its related considerations as it could be rendered in a Quiché-speaking household—and only possibly in Spanish. "I will argue," Stoll writes, "that the violence in Ixil country was not an outgrowth of local social struggle. Rather it was the result of insurgents choosing a backward area where state authority was weak. The predictable overreactions of security forces would help the guerrillas start a movement" (Stoll 1992: 64-65).[50]

Stoll asserts that in 1992 the 500 years of resistance was not commonly celebrated in Ixil. He writes that new Mayan alphabets mandated by Maya intellectuals, generated in opposition to the one chosen by the Summer Institute of Linguistics, did not stir the people in Quiché who were equally unaware that Menchú had been nominated for the Peace

Prize (Stoll 1993: 309). He uses this information as corroborative evidence for his assertion that the Ixils and their neighbors were not interested in participating in a revolution. Menchú has written that she did not know what was happening in towns within walking distance of her home until the disruption of her family. Further, Menchú left her homeland as a teenager, and was unable to return to Quiché for fear of death until after her award. In a rural and mountainous world where distance is covered primarily by foot, where few can read and there are no libraries, few books and almost no televisions or phones, these significant advances might well be unknown. How can they or anyone gauge the value of something if they do not know that it exists? The Nobel Prize is a Western gift spotlighting traumatic situations for Westerners, so that they can be monitored by outside interests. Stoll comments about a possible guerrilla comeback:

> This is why I have chosen to take at face value what Ixils say they want, which is peace. . . . To deconstruct their stated wishes in terms of resistance or a hidden transcript, or to argue that peace can be achieved only with justice as does the guerrilla movement can be used to impose an agenda for continued war. (Stoll 1993: 20-21, 126)

There is no reason to believe that every Mayan wants to be a revolutionary even though many hope for the changes that revolution could bring.[51] Nor could a war of the peasants anywhere be waged and won with sticks, even aided by some guerrilla leaders trained in Cuba, when the opposition was heavily funded by the outside, trained by the United States and armed to the teeth. Money was on the side of power. Wars do not start because guerrillas are trained; there are underlying causes. It seems valid to me to think that, as Stoll indicated, the Ixils wanted peace, especially after the insurgency. Yet, in contemporary theoretical reflection, prima facie information is precarious at best. There are other factors: a harmonious existence is part of indigenous ideology, and people cannot endure terror without compromise. Peace can be achieved without justice, by coercive force, as it was in Franco's Spain, but that is not to say that justice is not or should not be a pre-eminent goal.

Menchú wrote about the tentative peace agreement of March 30, 1991, in *El Clamor de la Tierra*:

> Nosotros vimos con simpatía el inicio de este proceso y manifestamos públicamente entusiasmo y voluntad de alcanzar el objetivo de la paz. Sin embargo, una auténtica solución no debe detener solo la guerra,

sino también atacar la injusticia social, la miseria, y la explotación que han llevado a la confrontación armada [We are sympathetic to the initiation of this process and we are demonstrating public enthusiasm and will to reach the objective of peace. It goes without saying that a real solution is not just stopping the war but also must attack the social injustice, misery and exploitation that caused the armed confrontation].[52]

As we will see in the process of this text, in the post-modern world, a unique sense of *self* is needed. When the *self* is annihilated or when the conditions in the contemporary world that incubate its development are destroyed, perverse things happen.

In Stoll's analysis we still have an almost classic replay of our first critique of Western ideology: it forces its conceptual world on things that have inherent forms of their own and in the wake of the disruption, decries the state of things and then endeavors to rescue its object. For Stoll, it did so by igniting warfare and then supporting guerrilla rescue teams or other military power. The culprits belong not only to the Right but also to the Left, and they are equally culpable in the standardization of difference. This created a situation in which the ideological positions of the Left and Right, maintained primarily by non-Mayans, have fought over the identity and control of a group of people who are not now and have not been honored in the discourse on their own life for hundreds of years.

We can assume that the Mayan possessed a home-based economy that was reasonably self-sufficient. Clothing, food and shelter were products of family endeavors. As their communal land became eroded through the encroachment of Mayan and non-Mayan outsiders, self-sufficiency in community was no longer a possibility. Other options for correcting deficits were examined on a variety of levels. These options included going to the coast to work, as well as finding religious or political solutions.

Víctor Montejo has explained that Maya did not understand *ideology*, and that some in his village and nearby believed that the far-off violence would remain distant from them because they were *good people*. Sadly this was not the way it turned out. Although Stoll acknowledges the historical oppression of the Maya of Guatemala, he seems to have little awareness of how the residuals of history affect thought processes or how thought processes are systematically affected by continued adversity, nor how personal assumptions color interpersonal, intercultural and inter-ethnic relations. Practically speaking, ideals recede as proxemics become threatened. Women who weave and care for children cannot take care of the fields when the men are at war. A family with adequate land, food, clothing and shelter is not as likely to risk it for change, because that change is not necessarily perceived as imperative. For many, change is not perceived as possible and endurance is valued. Risk-taking is contingent on temperament as well.

Families with a certain amount of leisure, well-being or exposure can begin to reflect on the *ideal* world, and may choose, bourgeois though they may be, to work toward change. None of this happens in a void. It happens interactively. It also intersects with the cultural and political agendas of other groups with varying effects in Guatemala and the United States and Europe.

Within the text of Menchú there is evidence that the process of understanding poverty and the reactions to it evolved because of interactions with other individuals, villages, the landowners and outside groups (including the church and some radical organizers). This process developed within the context of everyday relations, in much the same way as someone in the United States or France would develop an understanding of the world in which they exist. In North America, however, the media saturates us with information increasing our awareness of world events, even if it does not increase our ability to critique them. Menchú and her family lived on land that was not very productive, closer to the margins of existence, higher up in the mountains. Not everyone works their way through the model put forth in this text. In any event, the following quote of Stoll is valid on its face even if it is ambiguous in its implications, joining two assertions that do not necessarily anneal:

> Certainly the guerrillas appealed to Ixil grievances against *Ladinos*, but there is no sign that the grievances would have led to rebellion without the polarizing effect of guerrilla and army counter blows. To the contrary, there is considerable evidence that most Ixils would have preferred to stay out of the line of fire. (Stoll 1993: 309)

Stoll describes the guerrillas on their debut in Nebaj, Sunday, January 21, 1979:

> "So, this is the guerrilla army of the poor, finally they have appeared," townspeople said with anxiety and wonder. . . . According to one account they were mainly Indians, according to another mainly university students from the capital. . . . A North American detained by the guerrillas for a few hours recalls that most seemed young, inexperienced, and nervous, but she thinks that they were not local, nor heavily *Ladino*, nor simply *campesinos*.

> If each of the above accounts is accurate, they point to a very special social group that has provided the first recruits for more than one guerrilla movement in recent years: Urbanized, educated youth from indigenous backgrounds who return to the countryside to make revolution. (Stoll 1993: 61)

Víctor Montejo deals at length with the first sight of the "mythical image of guerrillas" when they entered towns in the Kuchumantan to hold meetings. They had *Ladinos* as leaders. Montejo cites a specific instance of a towns changed dynamics, directly attributed to the killing of a school teacher by the army during a fiesta. The town was radicalized. The teacher was Montejo's youngest brother. The date was February 1, 1981 (Montejo 1993: 96). He thereafter details the massacres by the military that he saw with his own eyes.

Montejo collected hundreds of hours of testimonies of survivors in Chiapas. He writes extensively in his dissertation about the subtleties of the problem, not the lack of it:

> In Guatemala the armed confrontation between the army and the guerrillas has precipitated the destruction of life and indigenous cultures. In this conflict, the Guatemalan army is definitely the most responsible for human rights abuses, but the revolutionary forces have also contributed, in a lesser degree, to human rights abuses in the western highlands of Guatemala.
>
> As the revolutionary movement extended . . . the Guatemalan army began to plan a major military action to counteract this expansion. In the army's view, the indigenous communities because they were poor, landless and marginalized would join and support the guerrillas. . . . The army made the indigenous communities the major focus of their counter-insurgency strategies. (Montejo 1993: 84-85)

David Stoll stated at the 1993 Latin American Studies Conference that the story of the torture of Menchú's brother, Petrocino, was fabricated, that others who witnessed the same scene said he was not tortured.[53] When Stoll, who is Menchú's antagonist, interviewed his witnesses, he did so in front of others. The presence of these officials makes this testimony suspect. And then there are the *disappeared*. Something happened to thousands of individuals: Rigoberta Menchú's brother, someone else's brother, Menchú's mother, someone else's mo-ther or child. We cannot neutralize the terror by localizing blame. The tragedy of even one person's death from torture is an indictment, not an admission of fabrication of life events.

Our inquiry into the nature of truth necessitates consideration of more than nonfiction. We need to look at verity. Testimonial literature tempers our understanding of *facts*, and comprises an invaluable resource in the social sciences, as in life, because the realm of the true is not the same as the realm of the provable. *Facticity* (our grasp of the facts) is not truth, which carries a greater, understandably deeper realization of the interconnection between action and perception and meaning.

Conversion-Aversion and the Protestant Missionary Position

One of the most dramatic contemporary occurrences has been the rise of Protestantism in Guatemala. Protestantism, in the form of evangelical churches, sects, cults and charismatics, has been influential in social change and that influence will affect the disposition of Mayan cultural process in later generations. Juxtaposed against skepticism of the postmodern world, it cuts a peculiar and discordant figure. Especially so because it has been rejected by so many Western-trained intellectuals and missionaries have been a source of colonial discourse for hundreds of years. Yet Protestants and postmodernists share the same irreverence for hierarchy. Protestant Christianity does not carry the same cultural baggage in Latin America as in the United States and Europe but may provide the same functions and have similar aims.

At the time of the first conquest of the Americas, the movement in Western Europe from Catholicism to Protestantism at the reformation was a movement toward audience participation, a flattening out of the hierarchy, resulting in the sainthood of all believers. Protestantism still offers the possibility of speaking, without the intermediary of a priest who does not live like *you*, directly to God, who hears and understands all things through prayer. Direct access to an omnipotent, omnipresent and omniscient deity (not a multinational corporation) who intercedes for us here and in the life after death, undercuts need for temporal mediation. It guarantees answers if the petitioner has faith and patience. Calvin's *Institutes of the Christian Religion* echoes, often anonymously and unidentified, as it assures Protestants that their chosenness by God will be manifested by their prosperity on earth, indirectly removing personal responsibility for failure or success.[54] An individual suffers only if destined to do so. For enduring this suffering, an individual is rewarded in the afterlife, eternity, in a place where no one can take the reward from you—through envy or revolution. This is a powerful emollient and persuasive medicine in an uncertain world.

Evangelical sects offer a correction for home lives deeply rived by culturally enforced alcoholism while charismatics offer a psychic release in the temporal world.[55] Charismatics, Catholic or Protestant, have the mystical trappings of the *cargoes* but they are associated with the new, not the traditional, and they provide a means of external expression and surrogate for those who cannot move away from home. The thrust of evangelical Protestantism, is both essentialist- and mission-based: it is one's responsibility to tell the lost of their condition, so they can repent (change their behavior). Under the language of love, the church has acted out its hegemonic power. In this sense it is similar to the mysticism of the original Franciscan missionaries in the new world. Protestant missionaries of different affiliations have been in Guatemala for a very long time. Because they speak metropolitan languages and are connected in many ways to social services, the secondary function of missions, and connected as well to the outside world, especially North America, they form a vital conceptual link in the connection between progress, technology and the west.

David Stoll sees a complex intertwining of ideas about the guerrilla war and the rise of Protestantism, bolstered by the military, by its order and enforced peace, by its Protestant evangelical generals but, as Stoll writes:

> What counts is a crucial difference: how Rios Montt replaced chaotic terror with a more predictable set of rewards and punishments, that is what passes for law and order under the country's normal level of repression. . . . Offers of amnesty were not what they were touted to be—folks were punished who did not take up the offer. (Stoll 1993: 111, 113)

A general tenant of Protestantism, given by Christ to the church is that one "render unto Caesar that which is Caesar's and unto God that which is God's," effectively prevents Protestant churches from participating in antigovernment activities. It also clearly establishes the binary opposition that was the cornerstone of modernism. The stance of the radical arm of the Catholic Church supports liberation theology, which encourages a temporal solution to these problems through social justice. Stoll intimates that Catholic Action was imported into Central America to keep parishioners in the Catholic church and foment revolution. While it certainly did these things, Catholic Action was worldwide and can count as its former members (years before) Freire, Foucault and Althusser—different sorts of revolutionaries altogether. That is not to say that liberation theology is solely the aegis of Catholics. Protestant theologians, like Jurgan Moltman, Miguel Bonino, Pixley in Argentina, Mortimer Arias in Bolivia and others, are deeply invested in these ideas as well, as a reaction to discourses that favor privilege.

It seems that the body of the Catholic Church and a number of its priests in Central America had little concern for or understanding of the needs and life of the indigenous populations they represented. Often priests did not speak the local dialect. Menchú spoke about this in her book. That is not to say that they did not think that they cared for the people, rather that they might not have loved them if they did not think that they could convert them.

The Summer Institute of Linguistics, a Protestant missionary organization, specializes in translating and preparing dictionaries of unwritten languages. These newly recorded languages are then used to translate the Bible. Clearly, the Protestant church uses effectively the connection between language and identity. This use of the connection constitutes a two-edged sword. On the thrust it honors the indigenous languages that were not honored under either the Latin mass or the Spanish one, while on the parry using them as a tool for evangelism.

Arias writes:

> Regardless of the external debate, Indian communities continued to search for new values to re-establish their commonality, their identity, and their place in the new environment. They sought a substitute for the ancient sacred bonds, now eroded by the rapid changes their communities had experienced, that could link self, neighbor, and place. (Arias 1992: 237-38)

Closed religious observances have necessitated the use of outside items, especially alcohol. As a result, interaction with *Ladinos* has increased. Even in this case there are tradeoffs. In some Mayan communities, *Ladinos* are entering the *cofradías*, which increases the indigenous base and gets *Ladino* money into the *fiesta* system. Concomitant with the rise in *cultos* and *evangélicos* is the rise of the practice of daykeepers, who maintain what they believe to be the original Mayan spirituality.[56] Roberto Poz Pérez, a daykeeper from Zunil told me that the rise of interest in Mayan spirituality is directly related to a rise in Mayan consciousness and the negative influence of the outside church as well as the broader availability of materials with which to train *sacerdotes*. He estimates that there are no less than five percent of Maya who devoutly maintain this form of spiritual practice.

In 1995, at the Mayan new year celebration in San Francisco, California, María del Carmen, a daykeeper from Sololá, came as celebrant for the services that were held for a mixed group of Maya and interested North Americans. In the remarks that preceded the ceremony, she said, "We are breaking our silence. The time has come for us to share our secrets with the world in the hope of peace. We believe we (Maya) understand things people here need to know." As Bakhtin so lyrically stated in *Speech Genres and other Essays*: "Every idea will have its homecoming." Things are changing—for all of us.

Part Two

Testimonies: Poetic Politics

But where are facts if not embedded in history and then reconstituted and recovered by human agents stirred by some perceived or desired or hoped for historical narrative, whose future aim is to restore justice to the dispossessed? Answers to these questions must reside in a theory of perception, a theory of intellectual activity and an epistemological account of ideological structures as they pertain to specific problems as well as to concrete historical geographical circumstances. None of these things is within the capacity of a solitary individual to produce; and none is possible without some sense of communal or collective commitment to assign then a more than personal validity.

Edward Said, "Permission to Narrate"

Me llamo Rigoberta Menchú and *Testimony: Death of a Guatemalan Village* show how a process of metamorphosis actualizes itself from the culture of silence into production of the written word as testimonial. These narrative/documentary testimonials are narratives of extremity because they represent and record events at the edge of consciousness. Repetitive violence affects the development of the self by arresting the imagination and repressing the ability to speak. These testimonials are not what Bakhtin calls "merely confessional self-accounting which has neither hero nor authorship in an interrelationship." What we see in these testimonials is "the spirit prevailing over the soul in the process of becoming and finding itself" (Bakhtin 1990: 100). They record the *lived horizon of being*. Now we need to examine how this process develops through the steps previously described, from silence to individual freedom. First, what do these testimonials tell us about the nature of oppression?

Absorption/Internalization of Outside Opinion about the Individual

Briefly, *Testimony: Death of a Guatemalan Village* is the retelling of events which transpired on a single day, September 9, 1982, in a small village where Víctor Montejo was the school teacher. Montejo's testimonial is a lethal parody of mistaken identities in which the members of the civil patrol of his village (every man who lives in a village is co-opted for certain periods each month to protect the village) mistake members of the Guatemalan army for guerrillas and fire on them. The result is that some army soldiers are killed. Many in the civil patrol are killed later by the army officers. Captured men are forced to confess knowledge of alleged misdeeds of their *compañeros*. Other innocent people (Víctor among them) are implicated by villagers being tortured who are trying to save their own lives. Montejo writes: "In that climate, anyone can condemn to death his own neighbor with the slightest accusation or rumor. It has become conveniently easy to get rid of a person for reasons of revenge and personal differences."[57] Threats of torture and death induce compliance and extreme paranoia. Montejo continues, "The army officers know they will rise in rank in accordance with the number of unfortunates they execute. It is a sort of rivalry encouraged among these officers who behave with such cruelty and savagery and destroy entire Indian communities without remorse" (Montejo 1987: 39). The violence here is gratuitous, unmediated.

Montejo's Response and Ethical Behavior

Víctor Montejo felt compelled to help the villagers in their resistance. Even though he is Maya, he was neither born in the village, nor did he live there. As the village schoolteacher, he was marginal in his participation in the affairs of the community. In the process of trying to help them, he was arrested and taken to jail. Following his release, he was forced to flee Guatemala. In an act performed through his status as *other,* Montejo speaks on behalf of the town to demonstrate to North Americans the violence taking place in Guatemala. By seeking to become the voice for the people in the village, the *fiduciary,* or as Miguel Barnet calls it, the *gestante,* he articulates the silence of the village and thereby defies the collective silence and oppression which are the leitmotif of the events retold in this testimonial. This silence needs translation and interpretation. The *understanding of the total experience* is Montejo's impetus for writing and for further actions on behalf of the village/other, as well. Montejo writes in his dissertation:

> Because I have been personally affected by the political violence against the Mayan population in Guatemala . . . and have experienced the bitterness of life in exile, I find it a moral responsibility to make evident the plight of my people in exile. . . . As an insider, my efforts are centered on the issue of how I can tell my collective story and at the same time elicit a strong commitment from anthropologists to promote issues such as social justice, self-determination and human rights.[58]

For Bakhtin, there are two types of empathetic reactions. *Pure empathy*, in which one loses the sense of one's self, is indiscriminate, containing no possibility for growth. "In pure empathy," Bakhtin writes, "one tries to merge totally with the suffering of another" (Bakhtin 1993:

17-19). Nothing is gained because both are incapacitated by the process, subsumed in or by another's ethos. *Aesthetic empathy* objectifies, and is a relational function of thinking and differentiation. Bakhtin emphasizes that empathizing must be followed by a moment of objectification. Therefore, although Montejo speaks and writes for the village as *other*, on another level he does it for himself. In these testimonials the act of writing is the act of objectification needed to fulfill Bakhtin's criteria for an aesthetic act.

When Víctor Montejo comes to the event/text as outsider/author, it is with an already developing sense of *self*, as well as a sense of his ethical responsibility. Ethical freedom (freedom of the will) is not just cognitive. It is "the freedom of having my performed action from being in me" (Bakhtin 1990: 119). Until we can separate ourselves from our *self* we are hopelessly bound to solipsism and isolation. Unable to visualize actions that are truly for the benefit of others, we are tied and bound solely to self-gratification and our erroneous belief in self-sufficiency. In this situation, we will never understand what it is like to be in someone else's shoes.[59] Ethical freedom is liberation. It promotes the ability to love and the ability to reach out. Bakhtin identifies this *ethical freedom* as the "mediator between the cognitive and ethical realms in any aesthetic creation" (Bakhtin 1993: 78).

Recognizing the "muteness and invisibility" of the villagers, Montejo assesses his responsibility toward the village. He writes: "It would have been cowardice to abandon this place which had suffered so terribly. . . . I don't know how I found the courage to try and save these endangered people" (Montejo 1987: 23-24). Montejo's reaction reflects what Bakhtin calls a "moral attitude of consciousness, which content ethics does not know." Víctor Montejo's decision is "something issuing from within [him]self—namely the morally *ought to be* attitude. *Ought* is precisely a category of the individual act—the category of individuality—of uniqueness and compellentness" (Bakhtin 1993: 28). Disembodied, literally scared out of his wits, Víctor Montejo is sentient. "I had not given much thought to my own situation until then. Only when they released the defender did I become aware that I had a rope around my neck" (Montejo 1987: 46). Víctor Montejo writes at the end of his story that after he was released:

> I spent the ensuing hours sunk in dark thoughts. To live like this, a plaything subjected to the whims of these people was not easy for a man with my yearning for peace and justice and freedom. I didn't know how long I could withstand it. I had my pride as a man of conscience,

at whatever cost. I had to endure with dignity the intense pressures I was being subjected to. These men could trick me with lies and false accusations and a thousand ruses they thought up themselves, but as long as I remained firm and serene, they could not make me fall easily into their traps. I would suffer with patience and humility. (Montejo, 1987: 104-105)

Silence and Its Meaning in Oppression

At this point we need to examine the relationship between muteness, invisibility and silence. Voice has both literal and figurative connotations, as an antithesis to silence and also as the vehicle for self-articulation. The voice of the *other* is not always silent, nor is it always mediated.[60] In *Testimony: Death of a Guatemalan Village*, muteness is synonymous with an undifferentiated *self.* Invisibility indicates the objectification of the *other*, and silence, which includes both these ideas at different times, can also indicate both wisdom and prudent behavior. For Freire, "Silence does not signify an absence of response, but rather a response which lacks a critical quality" (Friere 1987: 24).

In *The Problem of the Text,* Bakhtin iterates that the "absolute lack of being heard" is the absolute absence of a third party. In terms of his testimonial, Víctor Montejo functions as the invisible third party who stands above all the participants in a dialogue. He is "the constitutive aspect of the whole utterance who under deeper analysis can be revealed in it. For [a] work (and for a human being) *there is nothing more terrible than a lack of response*" (Bakhtin 1986: 117, 120).

The following examples demonstrate how Montejo records the village.

More members of the patrol arrived with their uniformed captors. They looked as if they had fled an insane asylum. . . . The defenders suffered in *silence.* At first I thought the captives would flee. But, they all remained *silent*, unmoving; only their faces expressed their confusion. Those poor young men had fallen into the hands of criminal soldiers, who acted without waiting to verify the source or the motive behind the lists they held in their hands. (Montejo 1987: 21)

Silence reigned in the village during those days. No one commented on the tragedy, and even the civil defenders distrusted one another. They confined themselves to complying with the army's orders to run up the flag every morning at six, and lower it at six every evening. For the rest, *everyone kept hermetic silence.* (Montejo 1987: 107)

How craven to betray a neighbor that way—far worse than killing him with weapon in hand. . . . At first I thought some of the captives would attempt to flee, but it did not turn out that way. They all remained silent, unmoving. (Montejo 1987: 39)

The process of reflection which in time produces a metamorphosis into personal freedom begins with the understanding that one is oppressed and the ability to name one's oppressor. Every oppressor needs a victim, writes Freire, in *Pedagogy of the Oppressed*, arguing that the oppressed develop a feeling of adhesion to their oppressors and are insufficiently self-delineated to "discover him [the oppressor], outside themselves. . . . One pole aspires to identify with the other" (Freire 1987: 30). The poles are in fact the two halves of the same construction. Mimetic behavior has a paradoxical relation with alterity. When people are offered an opportunity to become something which *seems* to be *other* than an oppressed, i.e. an oppressor, they accept it because they do not have sufficient understanding to allow them to see their position for what it is, merely an exchange of one type of oppression for another. In fact an *other* is no longer needed. *Individuals begin to oppress themselves.* Growth is toward the process of being, whereas these individuals are merely reflective of their present. "We have to obey the captain. The captain is always behind us. If we do not obey him, he shoots us. . . . We are not all the same, many of us have come to believe in what we are doing" (Montejo 1987: 148). A different view is presented by one soldier who remains behind to explain the plight of the others:

They deceived us into joining the army. It was against our wills. The fifty dollars they pay us a month is not enough to support our families with. That is why they allow us to loot and steal, so we can supplement our meager wages. We were tricked into coming here. The officers tell us we Indians must do away with our own people because the Indians are enabling the guerrillas to carry out the revolution. (Montejo 1987: 68)

Rigoberta Menchú writes, "We felt abused when they came and took our men, because we knew that although we might see them again they would never be the same. . . . It also means that an Indian soldier can kill other Indians" (Menchú 1984). Bakhtin writes that self-preservation is *always* cold and cruel (Bakhtin 1990: 48). Because it is a corruption of the process of self-definition and the catalyst in the fusion of the 'victim' with his oppressor, shame/humiliation can only be *abuse of the undifferentiated other, and the abnegation of an individual's responsibility to answer for himself.* Consequently, it is synonymous with rejection of one's own selfhood with regard to others. It is degenerative by its very nature. In this state, these villagers cannot know who they are. They have been deprived of a vocabulary/voice to formulate their consciousness. Their silence is hermetic because it seals off their feelings from concomitant actions. Menchú writes that when the soldiers came into Chajul bringing her brother and the others on lorries, everyone was enraged, but no one knew what they could do because they were afraid of a massacre. "We the people did not have the capacity to confront them. [The action was intended] to strike terror into the people and stop anyone from speaking" (Menchú 1984: 178). While they may dwell on their *selves*, or outwardly on their situation, terror and psychic trauma prevent them from acting on their own behalf. The villagers and soldiers who are indigenous are "victims of violence which has become institutionalized" (Montejo 1987: 88). The villagers reached out to Montejo (Montejo 1987: 23, 27).

Who Is Speaking?

While we see that the villagers do not speak, and Montejo makes a decision to speak, the officers and enlisted of the military are speaking. The dialogue between the civilians and the military delineates the attitudes of the military. Víctor Montejo's own voice when speaking with the military is a form of extreme politeness, "My Commander." On the other hand, the military sounds like this, "You old turd, if you open your mouth again, I'll fill you full of lead right here. An old bastard like you has no right to live" (Montejo 1987: 28). Or, "Speak up shit face," "as innocent as the great whore," "all right you fucker," "no pity for these motherfuckers." Montejo writes of himself, "*Mi comandante*, I beseech you to understand my situation." The military responds, "Shut up you piece of shit" (Montejo 1987: 43-44, 50). "Look, little schoolmaster, son of *la chingada*, don't you come off giving us any orders" (Montejo 1987: 44).

Relentless obscenity never gets anywhere. This audacious diatribe is mimetic, not generative. The interaction between the civilians and the military is collusive, a closed non-dialogic situation.[61] The language of humiliation is part of the process of oppression. "An indifferent or hostile reaction is always a reaction that impoverishes and decomposes its object" (Bakhtin 1993). Humiliation, an externally imposed shaming, causes psychic retreat and produces internal shame, the destruction of *self.* If there is a place for shame in Bakhtin's work, it is in doing without others, whether generated from inside or without.[62]

Live entering, as Bakhtin calls it, presupposes a self-defined individual who is capable of entering another (into his mind's eye, if you will) and seeing the life of another as that other sees it, without losing the sense of one's own agency or individual being.

Witness to the Executions:
Torture and Empathy

Let us visualize a situation in which we witness someone else's experience of physical pain. Bakhtin is to the point in discussing his *excess of seeing*. Here is his example:

> Let us say that there is a man before me who is suffering. The horizon of his consciousness is filled by the circumstance which makes him suffer and by the objects which he sees. He does not see the agonizing tension of his muscles, does not see the entire, plastically consummated posture of his own body, or the expression of suffering on his own face. Even if he [did] he would lack the appropriate emotional and volitional approach to these features. (Bakhtin 1990: 25)

Víctor Montejo and Rigoberta Menchú write about the torture they have seen. For them it is a literal *excess of seeing*, absorbed at the edge of consciousness. Montejo describes the torture that day:

> Señores, we are not going to demonstrate to you that we do not fear the guerrillas. Open your eyes wide, all of you, so you can see how we deal with the enemies of our government. We have been given orders to kill, and that is what we intend to do. (Montejo 1987: 46)

> For those who have to die, it is far better to be shot attempting to escape than to be killed slowly, staring up at our executioners faces as they cut you open. Fernando was cruelly tortured and then decapitated. They removed his teeth one by one and forced him to swallow them, like hard pellets. They cut off his tongue and pierced his eyes. (Montejo 1987: 85)

Rigoberta describes monstrous images detailing the death of her mother, her brother and her friends. These documentary images bring us into direct contact with the violence and trauma these individuals have witnessed. The details of her description, select pieces of information, come into focus in her mind as the festering scene of her brother's torture. Perhaps a photograph would have lent more 'truth value' for outsiders who have a difficult time imagining anything as heinous as what she endured. It might even have permitted Rigoberta Menchú to remain silent, since she would not have needed the words that she uses to describe the daily brutality of her existence. But catharsis occurs through moving from mental image to written word, articulating one's emotions. Describing exactly what she saw, as only she saw it, enables her to frame her reality for herself. It heals her, while it sets us on edge. She is not merely describing her anguish and pain so that we can live torment vicariously. She maintains control over her commentary on what she saw and felt. The commentary makes us responsible for the knowledge of the terror. We cannot objectify it. We cannot say as we might of a photograph, "Look, the soles of his feet are missing." We have to ask ourselves mentally, "What does a foot with no sole look like?" We visualize a gruesome detail. Menchú's graphic description follows:

> When I got closer to them, I saw that their clothes were damp. Damp from the moisture oozing out of their bodies. Somewhere around half-way through the speech, it would be about an hour-and-a-half, the captain made the squad of soldiers take the clothes off the tortured people. . . . They had marks of different tortures. This is a perforation of needles . . . this is a wire burn. . . . There were three people who looked like bladders . . . that's from something inside they do to hurt them. In my brother's case, he had no nails, he had no soles on his feet. A woman, one of her nipples was removed, one of her breasts was cut off, she had bite marks on different parts of her body. They poured petrol over each of the tortured. This is what we've done to subversives we catch. . . . This will happen to you. (Menchú 1984: 178-79)

> They were killing Keckchi Indians and the army massacred them as if they were killing birds—men, women and children. . . . We felt this was a direct attack on us. It was as if they'd murdered us, as if we were being tortured when they killed those people. (Menchú 1984: 160)

> We say that a person on his deathbed makes an inventory of his life. . . . As for killing someone: Death lived by others—be it death through an accident or any other kind—is something we feel very deeply, we feel it in our own flesh. (Menchú 1984: 202)

Death, strictly speaking, is not the problem of the one who dies. It remains the problem of the living who contemplate the death itself. Even the process of watching another die needs be objectified in the living for the living to keep functioning.

Rape and Women
and the Land

So far the discussion has centered on men in the army and men in the village. In *Testimony, Death of a Guatemalan Village,* however, there is a small inter-text about a woman whose son was killed. We understand by implication that because the women in the village are once-removed from the army, in that they are not forced into the civil patrol and are objects in the eyes of the military, that they are spared from mute and hermetic silence, although not from terror. Their external dependence means they can run for help; they can scream and they are still able to weep. In this way, ironically, the women have more power than the men. What about the women? Women are raped—internalization and invasion at its most literal—a denial of the *selfhood of an individual* by *another.* The testimony of Rigoberta Menchú delineates a complete cultural interrelation between the feminine, the land, the woman and the emotional exile from these beliefs engendered by the terrorism. Throughout both *Testimony* and *Me llamo Rigoberta Menchú,* rape is a synonym for the defilement of the sacred. The land, Heart of Earth, and the woman are sacred; both are feminine. This is one facet of the spiritual ethnography. Rigoberta writes:

> La tierra alimenta y la mujer da vida. Ante esa situación, la mujer tiene que conservar[lo] como un secreto de ella, un respeto hacia la tierra [The earth nourishes and the woman gives life. Understanding this situation, the woman must conserve this respect for the earth, as her secret]. (Menchú 1984: 198)

Contrast this with:

> [The girls who] had been raped by the army [were] pretty, humble girls. . . . They told me of their despair at having been raped. There were four of them. Two of them were pregnant by soldiers and the other two not. But they were ill, too, because they'd been raped by five soldiers who'd come to their house. . . . My friend told me, "I hate this child. This is not my child." . . . [S]he cried all the time. But I told her: "You must love the child. It was not your fault." . . . I didn't know what to do, I felt helpless. (Menchú 1984: 143)

In another place Menchú states, "The woman is the mother of the home and the earth is the mother of the whole world . . . the mother of all indigenous people" (Menchú 1984: 73). A bit further on she tells about certain social conventions which "preserve a woman's purity, which is something sacred, something special which will engender many lives" (Menchú 1984: 63). Víctor Montejo writes, "We had not gone far when a young woman raced towards us, pursued by a solider who clutched at her dress. She was pregnant, but that made no difference to the soldier who wanted to rape her" (Montejo 1987: 27).

Rigoberta writes about her friend Doña Petrona Chona's death at the *finca*:

> He began by asking her to be his mistress and to let him have his way with her. She kept saying, "No." In the end, he went away, but . . . that murderer sent someone to kill the woman in her house . . . to hack her to bits with a machete. We collected Doña Petrona up in baskets. Her head, her hands, her feet, all cut off. . . . Every time I remember it I get the same feeling. For six years afterwards, I dreamed about her. (Menchú 1984: 151)

Rigoberta speaks about her mother:

> They raped her. On the third day of torture they cut off her ears, they cut up her body bit by bit. They revived her so that they could torture her some more. They raped her some more, but she didn't die. My mother was covered with worms. They put her under a tree and left her with a permanent sentry so that no one could take the body away. (Menchú 1984: 198-99)[63]

In the mind of Montejo, the *campesino* is also synonymous with land. He writes that the village in which he taught shared all its land:

> The campesino feels that he is part of nature. He spends all his life bound to it like a bud or an unseverable and timeless offshoot. . . . All the Indians of this area share the lands in the traditional manner. The only land owners are outsiders who laid claims to tracts of land and took out documents. The vast majority live as their ancestors did, without private land ownership of any kind. (Montejo 1987: 57, 60)

Rigoberta writes that the first time the 'landowners' threw them out of their homes was in 1967.

> García's henchmen set out with ferocity. They were Indians too, soldiers of the finca. First they went into the houses without permission and got all the people out. Then they threw out all our things. . . . Everything broke. Those few days confirmed my hatred for *those* people. I saw why we said *Ladinos* were thieves, criminals and liars. They killed many of our dogs. They killed our animals. (Menchú 1984: 106)

Menchú's testimonial also deals with the sense of helplessness her people feel living and working at a *finca* on land which now belongs to non-indigenous people. One of the problems is the feeling of futility a person experiences when surrounded by strangers. Isolation is divisive because it destroys the fiber of community support. Indentured servitude causes a disjointed existence which results in social decay.

> Among them are people who've gone through a great deal. Mothers are very tired and just cannot do it. This is where you see the situation of the women in Guatemala very clearly. Mothers know that four of their five children could die. This terrible situation makes the men want to rebel, but they just try and forget because there is no other way out. (Menchú 1984: 36-37)

The *finca* represents not only the defilement of the sacred, but the usurpation/appropriation and occupation of these formerly native lands by outsiders, internal colonialism. The problem is not just one of being invaded, as it were in one's own village, and having one's land taken away, but being forced, because of the appropriation of one's homeland, to go and work in the fields of another. These folk are doubly displaced.

Conclusion

This section presents a bleak picture of souls under siege. Bakhtin calls the soul the "spirit as seen from the outside" (Bakhtin 1990: 100). First, this section illustrated that these villagers endure physical abuse and terror in an environment of hermetic silence. We can conclude that destruction of the fiber of life and culture produces social disequilibrium, because of the way it disrupts and eradicates continuity and prevents thinking. Generations of upheaval have resulted in the eradication of precedents which existed for salvific behaviors.

> How sad it is when a man loses his own identity and is easily indoctrinated. The defender was repeating to his own neighbor what the military drummed into his head: "Destroy, kill, even if it includes your own family." This military doctrine had gradually undermined the foundations of an indigenous culture, causing the Indian to act against his own will and best interests and destroying what is most sacred in his ancient Mayan legacy: love and respect for one's own neighbor, which translates into a policy of mutual support. (Montejo 1987: 63)

This section also demonstrated that the process of writing one's life is a catharsis that allows an individual who has suffered intensely to grow and go on living. As readers, *excess of seeing* can subvert the querulous negative observation, "Why don't they do something about their situation?" and replace it with, "How could they endure? How did they manage to survive?" Some can and do. As we saw with Víctor Montejo, and will see in detail with Rigoberta Menchú, in some individuals there is a unique intersection of will, reflection and opportunity. These survivors exist at the seams on the borders between consciousnesses that produce change.

Assessment of the *Self* Relative to Outside Influence

The assessment of the self requires first situating one's *self* ideologically. It also includes critical reflection about and reconciliation with the different aspects of one's life. This is the beginning of theory, the examination of assumptions which engage the cultural activity of a society.

Reconciliation has two aspects. The first is the assessment of what others have said about an individual (what that individual has internalized from what in this case is primarily non-Mayan sources). The second is the assessment of the individuals with respect to what they have learned about their own culture, from, in this case, Mayan sources. Which things will be useful to the individual in her growth? What things has the *outsider* declared that have merit? In other words, when individuals look at their belief systems and cultural heritage, how does it match what the *other*s are telling them about themselves? What we see is the selection and processing of information, a movement from indiscriminate feeling of betrayal by an anonymous *other* toward the discrimination that individuals differ. Bakhtin writes that man in general does not exist, but the totality of universal knowledge defines man in general. The masses are only the crowd beyond *one*. In the testimony of Rigoberta Menchú we can see what Víctor Montejo demonstrated in his response to the people in the village where he was the teacher, "To live from one's *self* does not mean to live for one's *self*" (Bakhtin 1993: 19).

Reconciliation with the External World

Rigoberta Menchú writes at the beginning of her narration that her experience is the experience of a whole people. What has happened to her is the story of all poor Guatemalans. But in a very real way, her experience is different. After her assessment of her situation and the situation of her *comadres*, she decides to do something about her situation. This is contrary to the situation which Montejo describes as characteristic of the behavior of the *others* in the village where he taught. Rigoberta Menchú writes:

> I started thinking about my childhood, and I came to the conclusion that I hadn't had a childhood at all. I never was a child, I hadn't been to school, I hadn't had enough food to grow properly, I had nothing. I asked, "How is this possible?" I began learning about politics. I tried to talk to people who helped me sort my ideas out. . . . Experience gave me a lot to think about. I have to tell you that I didn't learn my politics in school. I just tried to turn my own experience into something which was common to a whole people. I was happy when I found out that I wasn't the only little girl to have worried about not wanting to grow up. We were all worried about the harsh life awaiting us. (Menchú 1984: 117-18)

She records that "a nun asked a little boy if they were poor and he said, 'Yes, we are poor but at least we are not Indians.' It was painful for me to accept that an Indian was inferior to a *Ladino*. I kept worrying about it. It is a big barrier that they've sown between us" (Menchú 1984: 119). "We realize in Guatemala there is something inferior and something superior. Apparently there was a time when the *Ladinos* used to think we weren't people at all but a sort of animal" (Menchú 1984: 123).

When Rigoberta was about ten years old her little brother died while the family was working on the *finca*. "From that moment I was angry with life and afraid of it, because I told myself, 'This is the life I will lead too, having many children and having them die.' Those 15 days at the *finca* I remember with enormous hatred. *That hatred has stayed with me to this day.*" (Menchú 1984: 41).

On the occasion of her last visit to the *finca* Rigoberta writes, "So there I was with this problem of *how to find a way out of this life.*" Her sister took a job as a maid but could not stand up to the abuse. Rigoberta reasoned, "How could it be harder than our work because I always thought that it would be impossible to work harder than we did. So, why put up with it. I wasn't yet thirteen" (Menchú 1984: 90).

Reconciliation with Cultural History

Rigoberta Menchú records the history of her family's suffering in the context of cultural history. She deals with the heritage of her people and then with the political reality of being indigenous to Guatemala, moving between details of cultural practice and the personal aspects of her life and her spiritual ethnography. Rigoberta Menchú tells us in her testimonial that what she details about her culture is not about the *real* world per se but about *our reality*—a concept far larger. This is what I have called *sentient historicity*. It is based on cultural precedent rather than data. Sentience is interpretative because it implies an ability to feel and to reach out, grasp, and therefore understand.

Víctor Montejo recorded for outsiders and for cultural posterity the fables and stories repeated in his community. "By writing down these stories I am contradicting the myth of backwardness that has been created for us. So, in a way, writing is a kind of resistance."[64] Montejo writes that for him these fables are also a testimony to the respect, unity, and understanding between people and their natural and supernatural environments. The delineation of this relationship is another aspect of the spiritual ethnography. The continuous active participation of Mayan people in their tradition is an insistence against the corrosion of time. This insistence occurs as an act of preservation of ancient cultural traditions that were part of the heritage of Montejo and his people. These traditions are jeopardized by the act of learning to read, which reduces reliance on oral tradition; by metropolitan migration, which can hasten assimilation; and by cultural genocide, which has forced many Mayans into exile.[65]

There cannot be a transcription of fables and stories (folklore), or testimonials, without an individual who can speak and write. Víctor Montejo points out that most Mayans cannot read, and education, when it is available, is minimal. Montejo's translator, W. Kauffman, recorded that when Víctor Montejo was asked, after he came to the United States, what he had thought he might become as an adult, he replied that the prospect of education was so foreign to his hopes that it had never occurred to him that he would be any different from his father, a man who worked the land (Montejo 1987, n.p.).

Written language as text assumes the availability of an individual to productively transpose the form of mythic material so that it can be made available to a wide audience. In the case of these myths and stories, the best interpreter is the one who comes from the culture where the stories originate and believes in the preservation of that cultural ideal. Not simply from one language to another, these translations are of entire theoretical structures. Rigoberta Menchú reflects on the forms that help her and us to make sense out of her life. Practical survival is enhanced by the world view depicted in both Rigoberta's cultural accounting and Víctor Montejo's transcriptions of *The Bird Who Cleans The World* and *El Kanil*.

Possessing the ability to write is not enough. To be understood, language patterns and discourse styles within different communities would also need to be similar. There are cultural differences to be considered. Certain concepts and traits are culture bound, endemic to the culture of origin. Hence, what we need is not just the word *maize* transposed into another language as *corn*, but a coherent and cohesive concept placing itself in reality. We need to understand what is behind the *ear*—behind and also larger-than. What are the cultural implications behind the object/word? We need to understand the context of the words as well. The exchange of money for corn as food, for example, shows us deeper and expanded connections. We need to understand that corn is seed. As phallus or signifier it symbolizes the ability to come to fruition, die, and be reborn as food in the agricultural cycle, mystically in the *Popol-Vuh*, and symbolically, as emancipation in the works of Rigoberta Menchú. In *Philosophy of the Act*, Bakhtin writes that "historically, language grew up in the service of participative thinking and performed acts. It begins to serve abstract thinking only in the present day of its history" (Bakhtin 1993: 38).

Oral language continues even when written words are repressed. The stories continued to be told and remembered beyond the oppressive situation in Guatemala for at least two reasons. The first reason: the stories of the Maya are sequestered in their minds, preserved through the oral tradition. The second: published as books to be read elsewhere in the West, they communicate with another world. Bakhtin uses the concept of *signature* as an equivalent to valuation and claiming the written word/work as one's own. Víctor Montejo's transcriptions have produced texts that are simultaneously collective and authored, the offspring of a collective consciousness. The storyteller, who is the intermediary and an interpreter in the oral tradition, is replaced by the written word as text. By publishing these fables and the epic *El Kanil*, Montejo has claimed these stories for his people, and carried them from oral history to the written word, from the Mayan people to the world. This is the voyage of the *word* into the *world*. It begins the conscious development of a canon of national literature for the Mayan people.

Cultural Continuity and Symbolism in Myth and Epic

The continuity of fables and figures in dreams and myths binds people to their community and reflects their relationships and values, while placing the future in the present. Bakhtin writes that every *serious contemporaniety* requires an authentic profile of the past, an authentic other language from another time. Myth makes sense out of life. Memory rather than knowledge serves as a source and power for the creative impulse. Bakhtin reflects that literature is an inseparable part of the totality of culture and cannot be situated outside the total cultural context. It cannot be severed from the rest of culture and related directly (bypassing culture) to socioeconomic or other factors (Bakhtin 1986: 140).

In *The Bird Who Cleans the World*, Montejo sets down fables told to him by his mother. Without going into too great detail, it is possible to relate and apply the story that gives the book its name. The narrator gets right to the memory/heart of the matter. It is said that even the vulture, who, according to fable was sent out to see if flood waters were receding, stopped to gorge himself on the carrion he found and was late returning. Even Usmiq, the buzzard, who failed in his mission and must therefore forever clean the earth of contamination, curses what the White Man did to the sacred corn fields. The implication is clear: the devastation as a result of the Conquest was so great that even the buzzard in his greed could not clean it up. The buzzard, now a twice-failed bird, remains connected to carrion and waste. From this story we also learn that although the buzzard defecates on his feet, he keeps them from getting infected when he walks. He has no nest and his eggs are laid in caves. Nonetheless he has a special and crucial task; he is the environmental manager. The concepts at issue here are understanding of sense and place, a sense of the past, cultural attitudes toward the white man and what constitutes defilement of the sacred. The decimation of the cornfield by the white man is sacrilege because corn is holy. Rigoberta Menchú recounts for us the planting ceremony at the beginning of the corn cycle:

> The fiesta starts months before when we asked the earth's permission to cultivate *her*. Before seeds of corn are sown in the ground, we perform a ceremony. We choose two or three of the biggest seeds and place them in a ring, candles representing earth, water, animals, and

the universe that is *man*. In our culture the universe is man. The seed is honored because it will be buried in something sacred—the earth (*la tierra*)—and because it will multiply and bear fruit the next year. We do it mainly because the seed is something pure, something sacred. For us the word *seed* is very significant. . . . *Maize* is the center of everything for us. It is our culture. The *milpa* is the maize field. *Maize* is the grain. (Menchú, 1987: 53-54)

Rigoberta Menchú recounts the history of her people in much the same way as the narrator in *El Kanil*. She writes:

Nearly everything we do today is based on what our ancestors did. This is the main purpose of the elected leader—to embody the values handed down from our ancestors. He is the leader of the community, a father to all our children, and he must lead an exemplary life. Above all he has a commitment to the whole community. Everything that is done today is done in memory of those who have passed on. It is also when they remind us. We recreate the past through narrative and ceremony. (Menchú 1984: 13,17)

When Rigoberta told how her community maintained its cultural heritage, at the ceremony for reaching ten years of age, she wrote:

It is also then that they are reminded that their ancestors were dishonored by the White Man through colonization. The Spanish dishonored our ancestors' finest sons, the most humble of them. It is to honor these people that we must keep our secrets. No one except the Indians must know. They talk a lot about our ancestors. Children are reminded that they must respect their elders, even though this is something their parents have been telling them since they were little. (Menchú 1984: 13)

When she was old enough to travel and to organize, Rigoberta Menchú writes that it was her job to explain to different groups that the oppression that they were having to endure was not their fault. It was imposed on them by *Ladinos* (the outside world). That, she says, is why the *Ladino* world is disgusting. In an undiscriminating or unquestioning person, myths of origin merely lay blame, if they are used as an excuse for the unsatisfactory present. Here, the conquest is favored over advocating of personal responsibility. However, we note how this perspective modified itself as Rigoberta Menchú's understanding and experience broadened. It did not alter the past. However, it tempered her practice of the present, and her hope for the future.

Because cultural observation informs the practice of the present, we can look in greater detail at the story of *El Kanil: Man of Lightning*, one epic from oral history that has successfully descended into the written word. *El Kanil: Man of Lightning* is the story of a boy called Xuan, who gives his life for his people. The willingness to give one's life for another is a thread common in indigenous thought. The stance of the indigenous world is propitiation, in varied forms. The historical context for the beginning of the problems depicted in *El Kanil* is attributed also to the White Man and what transpired when the corn was desecrated.

Aun los zopilotes maldicen confusos
aquel cruento día lejano y fatal
en que los invasores blancos y ambiciosos
despojaron al gran cacique Jich Mam
de sus fértiles tierras y maizales.

¡Oh!, que pequeños somos hoy en casa
ante la grandeza de nuestros abuelos;
aquellos héroes mitad hombres, mitad dioses
que incansables abrieron brechas luminosas
en el corazón de la noche perpetua
para leernos un paraíso de tórtolas
que han de arrullarnos como vírgenes
junto con los clarividentes clarineros
"negros espías del tiempo"
que ordenan a las nubes que llueva. (Montejo 1982: 4)

[Even the vultures curse the bloody day
when white men ravaged the good lands
and cornfields of the chief Jich Mam.

Today we live like children in the house
of our great ancestors: heroes, half-gods,
who in the heart of everlasting night
tore great luminous breaches and bound us
to heavens full of doves that sing out
like maidens beside the clear-eyed trumpeters,
the dark spies of the seasons
who order the clouds to rain.]

Poetically, the sections of *El Kanil* present the following structural elements:

Portico: The symbolic washing to prepare to enter the presence of the sacred.

Section I: The history of the gifts for a good life given by Jich Mam and Jich Mi, first mother and first father. We read what life was like in this idyllic state.

Section II: Community is the cornerstone of the people: "The past is today's food and tomorrow's honor. Not one of us can be what we all are not. . . . The same straw covers all our roofs." This section also tells of the first diaspora, and how the old gods pissed in the packs and baskets and stole away to caves like wounded moles and old toads after the first volcanoes. The search for a new way to be in the world and the move to a new location. The section culminates with the closing of the circle of the twelve guardians (K'ues) around their promised land, Jacaltenango (Xajla'). The old gods still grumble even though they have been replaced, so memory of the past lingers even when it has been dismissed.

Section III: The plentitude of the spiritual aspect of culture; the use of healers and how their power "drove the dark spirits away and the sickness that stole among us and demanded lives." At the first warning of the peril to come, the owls, "who see in time through darkness," laughed at their approaching destiny.

Section IV: Jich Mam chooses the strongest, the most devoted and especially the brave to defend the people.

Section V: The sorcerers argue for their abilities to change into animals and insects and demonstrate their skills. Jich Mam allows the twenty-eight sorcerers to replace the brave, knowing that they may be killed. The text indicates parenthetically here that at this time Matzualil, the devil, walked among them, striking them down with disease and madness. Perhaps this is included to indicate how the sorcerers became so puerile, perhaps as a explanation for the inappropriate behavior in a group which was meant to be so idyllic in its composition. In either case, the best stay behind to insure cultural continuity. The two water boys are chosen.

Section VI: Xuan's meeting with all the gods the night before they leave is described here. He visits one mountain after another and asks for the right kind of power to help his people. After his blessing he jumps up and rubs his hands in satisfaction.

Section VII: The group sets out. The sorcerers are full of themselves and belittle the porters. Xuan quietly carries his power and the packs (a double meaning of the word *cargo*).

Section VIII: Juan Méndez, the second porter, is initiated into the understanding of the use of light.

Section IX: The transformation/conversion of two sorcerers who acknowledge the true power of Xuan.

Section X: On the scene, one warrior tells the king that they "began to fight when we left Xajla'," so they will complete their mission. Xuan and Juan, alone on the shore, are met by a "brother from Chiapas" who dreamed of their need and came to help. The king intervenes to save a few of those who were left so that nothing will be eradicated and no knowledge will be lost. The victory is made but the sorcerers refuse to celebrate. "Our men turned their backs on their honors, preferring the peace of humility to all the world's feasts and celebrations." They begin the return home, changed.

Section XI: As the troop comes within sight of the town, Xuan and his companions lag further and further behind. Because they have used their power in a slaughter and have violated the peace of their community, they are not able to return to live among their people. Xuan promises that in future danger, their "banners will fly in the clouds and their voices will speak in the wind, always." The sorcerers are reduced to "skulking dogs or crying children." "We conquered, but the victory belongs to the carriers and the lightning man from Chiapas, Juan Carmelo." Xuan and his compañeros are transformed into a mountain at which to celebrate the event, and the villagers burn copal. "Though we hear and see nothing, we feel their breath and their words."

Bakhtin writes that what is important in the epic is not the factual sources, not the content of historical events (in this case, invaders from the sea, who can spin silk and have strange weapons). Folklore interprets and saturates space with time and draws it into history. What is important is that the epic represents a sacrosanct point of view (Bakhtin 1981: 16). Rigoberta Menchú has called this point of view *her reality*. Xuan knows that if he accepts the gift of lightning he will not be able to return to his people, he will be changed. His decision to do something is made before he goes to B'alun C'ana, the first of the lightning men. B'alun C'ana tells him that his lightning is so strong it would leap from Xuan's hands and destroy the world. Xuan visits another mountain and another, each with power too strong or of the wrong sort for him. At last he arrives at El Kanil, the one who, leaning down from his cloud cover asks him benevolently, "How can I help you?" The allegory here is related to the actual use of light and subsequent enlightenment, and the responsibility for the good of others, which is inherent in the use of light. The reward for the proper use is ironically the separation of the user from his cohorts and family, and his initiation into the cosmic canon. The town is not defiled by the presence of those who have experienced violence, something that obsesses both Menchú and Montejo in their testimonials. In *El Kanil*, Xuan is made into a mountain, returned again to the male extension of the mother earth. This transformation more closely resembles a Western idea of transfiguration and sainthood than super heroism. It cannot be viewed as a suicidal martyrdom because it is not an act of aggression on his *self*. It is a story of decision, growth and reclamation, and reinstatement. His act has powerful and positive repercussions on the people whom he leaves behind. This is how Víctor Montejo described Xuan's encounter with the gods:

> Xuan ran leaping like the deer through the hills,
>   running south to the magnificent K'anil.
> The great K'u leaned over him like a cloud.
>
> Xuan shouted, "Give me your powers, great K'anil."
> K'anil answered, "Xuan tell me why you ask."
>
> "Tomorrow my brothers go to fight a war
>   for a dying people far from here.
> Their messengers followed our fame to Xajla'.
> Their enemy fights only from the sea,
>   protected by the waves and strange weapons.
> Our battalion that leaves in the morning is not warriors but sorcerers.
> They can turn themselves into vicious beasts and strange pests,
>   but what will they be on the beach
>   but more targets for the invader's arms?
> We will all lose our lives by that sea."
>
> "Father K'anil," Xuan begged, "I want to save them
>   I don't care if I never return."
>
> The great K'u heard this story and said, "Are you ready to abandon all
>   you have and never change your mind?"
>
> "I have made the choice forever," Xuan answered. (Montejo, 1982:37)

Xuan is given a yellow shirt which holds all the powers he has asked for. He goes along to the battle as the waterboy, carrying the packs. "Xuan, con la pesada carga sobre la espalda callaba sus *secretos*, ocultaba sus poderes." (Conversely, during the Inquisition in the Americas the *sanbenito* worn by the heretic on his way to his *auto de fe* was also yellow, embroidered with symbols of satan and the wearer's unrepented sins.)

Another of the virtues/powers of Xuan is his ability to keep his own council and not reveal the secrets that he knows. His composure is complete. Xuan is indeed a special child who, knowing that he has the power to eradicate an army, never tells anyone, only bites his lip and keeps his peace. This theme of secrets is also very evident in Rigoberta Menchú's narrative. The narrative of *El Kanil* reveals that those who saw Xuan straining with the packs saw nothing, save a silent young man. They did not know that they walked with a K'u. The travelers did not understand how they survived.

> Death itself ruled the path on which they traveled.
> Wolves howled after them and the big cats stalked the slowest porters.
> Those who led the way cut through spiny thickets,
>   stepped on waiting snakes.
> They crossed rivers and gorges and jungles.
> The rains drenched them and the heat sucked their strength while
> Death, imitating the shrill monkeys, threw rocks and fruits
>   from the thick tree tops. (Montejo 1982: 41)

Bakhtin refers to the space provided in epics for the intrusion of non-human forces that act through the hero as *adventuristic time* (Bakhtin 1981: 95). The epic hero enters *adventuristic time* as a person to whom something happens. But the initiative in this time belongs to human beings. In *El Kanil* we can see this developed. Xuan is reflective and he not only initiates the action, he shares his understanding and completes his work. Xuan subverts through humility, a trait characterized by reflective behavior and an understanding of place. When he and the other wise child have finished their practice, consisting of splitting trees with lightning bolts until they split perfectly in two halves, Xuan replaces all the trees, so there is no damage to the earth. It is restored. His priority is not himself.

In the *Philosophy of the Act*, Bakhtin writes that one can perform a political act or a religious ritual in the capacity of a representative, but that already constitutes a specialized action, which presupposes the fact that someone has been empowered to perform it. Even here one cannot abdicate personal answerability. "The tacit presupposition of life's ritualism is not humility but pride" (Bakhtin 1993: 52). To attempt to understand our whole life as a secret representation, or the act we perform as a ritual act, turns us into impostors, pretenders, or clones. Ritualism is associated with mimesis. As we saw in *Testimony: Death of a Guatemalan Village*, mimesis is not only copying; it is also bonding. The sorcerers in *El Kanil*, the people who are invested with *life's ritualism* are indeed characterized by their overweening pride. While Xuan is in the woods sharing his secret powers with another wise child, the sorcerers, seeing the results of Xuan's training—lightening and thunder and no rains and darkness at day—are each claiming the occurrences to be the result of their own power even as they are quarreling among themselves. Their pride is hubris; they only fool themselves.

Víctor Montejo writes another tale of J'ich Mam, the first father, in a story not commercially available. This tale, *The Disobedient Boy*, deals with a bad child who laughed when an old man, whom he asked for help, told him that no one would love him if he continued his disobedience. When the old man takes him in, we hear a story reminiscent of Italy, Strega Nona. Given the pot to watch, the bad boy puts in more than the thirteen beans he was directed to cook. The result is a disaster of many beans and a broken pot. On the second day, this same child is given another task with another caveat, which he does not mind. The fearless and heedless child opens "enormous covered water jars, behind a small door." The first spews great clouds of smoke, bringing thunder. He opens a trunk near the jug and puts on a red cape. This turned the child into thunder. The old man upon returning, sensing the problem, went to the trunk and put on a green cape. With this cape he calms the storm. The remaining cape of yellow is never used. Xuan gets a yellow shirt when he allies himself with El Kanil. The purple shirt of Caj'e, "where the sun hides at night," is too much for him. The bad child returns to his parents, and obedience. Xuan, after his work with the power-laden yellow shirt, is transformed (Montejo 1989).

Xuan is not alone in the canon of Mayan myth. Q'anil is one of the four year bearers in the Mayan calendric system. Lightning men are cited in the *Popol-Vuh* as names given to the Heart of Heaven. In the Annals of the Kaqchikel, a man of lightning arrives to liberate the Kaqchikel from Pedro de Alverado. K'anil has a long lineage as protector—in myth and in the contemporary world. K'anil is the protector of those villagers who are forced into the army in *Testimony: Death of a Guatemalan Village*. Montejo writes in the forthcoming new edition of *El Kanil* that women asked to be given the power of light, in the Tzotzil and Tzeltal uprising of 1712 (in Chiapas). Montejo traces the lineage of K'anil through many incidents in the life of his own family. For the Jakaltek Maya, Montejo writes, the tradition of K'anil is as vital as mother' milk, the breath of their being.

Reconciliation with Religion

> Guatemalans are the chosen people of the New Testament.
> We are the new Israelites in Central America.
>
> E. Rios Montt

> The speaking subjects of high proclamatory genres
> —of priests, prophets, preachers, patriarchal fathers—
> have departed this life.
> They have been displaced by the writer.
>
> M.M. Bakhtin

Rigoberta Menchú recounts that when she was younger, she did not have any idea what she was praying in church, because the prayers were not in Quiché, or Spanish, but Latin. "So, when we said something to express our faith, we didn't always understand what it meant" (Menchú 1984: 81). In the sense that Latin was understood by no one, neither *Ladino* nor Mayan, it was a more egalitarian language.

She writes that the ideas in Christianity, insofar as they taught her about the sacred and about faith and about the existence of God, were nothing new. Her culture already enforced a belief in the sacred and the nature of God. She understood the nature of piety. The act of prayer was enough. Catholicism merely reinforced an already active faith and spiritual consciousness. "This is why we maintain the rites for our ceremonies, and why we don't accept Catholic Action as the only way to God, and why we don't perform only Christian ceremonies" (Menchú 1984: 171).

Menchú parted company with Catholic doctrine when it separated the reality of heaven from the reality of suffering on earth. "Our *reality* teaches us that as Christians we must create a church of the poor—that we don't need a church imposed from outside which knows nothing of hunger. . . . It seems to me that the church wants us to believe that there is a wonderful heaven for the poor so that we must accept our life on earth" (Menchú 1984: 133). Rigoberta writes that unless religion springs from within the individual himself it is the weapon of *the system*. Besides, Rigoberta Menchú says, theologians have missed the point: "Han llegado teólogos, y que han visto y que sacan otra concepción del mundo indígena" [The priests came to see us, but they got another/a different conception of the indigenous world] (Menchú 1984: 42).

As Rigoberta Menchú became critical of the social superstructure of the church, she maintained her sense of the value of being Catholic and her affinity for scripture, because she perceived it as a model for revolutionary action in which she temporally is engaged. It is interesting to me that in not separating herself from her roots she is able to use scripture as a mosaic to frame her narrative. Her judgments are affected by her understanding of the human spirit in both religious and non-religious ways. Menchú reviews in her testimonial the religious leaders that she has seen: the nuns who don't answer her questions and the priests who tell her that she must suffer here on earth in order to have a rewarding afterlife in heaven. She notes, "Not all priests are people who can't see the reality and suffering of the people. Many of them love the people and, through this love for the people, they may love each one of us and help us show our people the way" (Menchú 1984: 162).

Bakhtin relates in *From the Prehistory of Novelistic Discourse* that in the middle ages the primary appropriation was that of the scriptures. He states that in other times these appropriations were the space for heroism which changed and developed until the individual herself through her self-reflection and delineation was able to see herself as the hero of her own life.

Speaking for her people, Menchú has a preferential option for the context of community, and a belief system which is consistent with her perspective. "We don't need a king in a palace," she declares, "but a brother who will live with us" (Menchú 1984: 134). She suspects that the hierarchical church is tainted by the same ideas and groups that have brought oppression to her people. Theology is a different matter. It is a personal, interpretive issue. It is not retrospective for her, nor does it deal with propitiation for sin as such, but deals with destiny. By using it she validates once again the future and present using the past without becoming mired in it. As a narrator, Menchú has become a prophet and evangelist of the new gospel of the poor. Behind Rigoberta are the mystical metaphors of her culture, the scripture stories of Judith and Moses, and the rhythm of the Exodus. In her future is emancipation. Her vision is not just for herself but for an entire people. Both theology and metaphysics present an order beyond time. The stories from Menchú's cultural heritage and the Catholic scripture reinforce the belief that in simple acts of faith reside revolution and reform. "The important thing for us is that we started to identify that reality [the stories of the Old Testament] with our own" (Menchú 1984: 131), not the other way around.

The story of Judith was written perhaps at the time of the Macabees, placing it in the transitional period between the transcription of the Old and New Testaments. So, this story is a bridge between two ways of seeing the world. To see why Judith is especially fitting for Rigoberta Menchú personally, as Moses is a redolent symbol for the Mayan people, we need to review the story line from the Apocrypha. Nebuchadnezzar, who was thwarted by the lack of Hebrew support during war time, sent General Holofernes to lay siege to their city, Belthulia. The Hebrews resisted until the water supply was cut off and contaminated. They were advised by their sages to bow to Holofernes. Judith, a beautiful widow of great piety, upbraided the people, saying: "If you cannot vanquish them, I shall do it myself." Whereupon, she went to Holofernes in his camp and seduced him with drink. While he was inebriated, she took his sword and cut off his head, which she brought back to the city in a bag. The head was publicly displayed. Her act encouraged the Hebrews to advance against their assailants. The story ends with the thanksgiving hymn of Judith. Judith crystallizes the image of the individual who Rigoberta Menchú is becoming. This story represents a different archetype from the story of Moses. There is a heroine rather than a hero. Judith is reflective. She chooses and acts. She uses what she has: beauty and courage. Her experiences must clearly have rung true for Rigoberta Menchú. Judith is a widow. War widows are a commonplace in Guatemala. In a patriarchal society, a woman without a husband has no purchase. Where Judith may have been brave because she had nothing to lose because she was alone, she was still beautiful, still marriageable. Being alone meant that she *had* to do for herself. Her life was characterized by its reverence and the practical practice/application of her faith. Rigoberta sleeps with dreams of what happened to Doña Petrona Chona. What if Doña Petrona Chona had reversed the situation and had taken her assailants head?

"We all became Moses," Menchú states. Referring back to the first section of this text we can see strong Moses comparisons between the Old Testament and *El Kanil*. If *El Kanil* is a pre-Conquest document, it may have been super-synchronistically affected by Christian themes brought by the missionaries. In any case, we can see how Xuan, a child, went directly to God and asked for the power to overwhelm the enemy.

Xuan was worthy because he chose. He had insight. Moses was chosen *by* God. God came to *him* in a burning bush and said, "Take off your shoes, you are standing on holy ground." Moses is a prototype of annunciation, not initiative. Xuan went to El Kanil because he clearly understood that the sorcerers would die because they were motivated by pride, or an undifferentiated *self*. He said to El Kanil, "What good will be accomplished if you turn your *selves* into vicious beasts on the beach? They will be targets for the invader's arms." He received a yellow shirt, a special *traje* and the power to throw lightning bolts. Moses threw his staff and it turned into a snake. In the desert, he hit rocks and water came out. Moses seems like an underdog, an abandoned child who stammers. In reality he was a patrician who had been hidden by his mother to avoid the pogroms against the first born. He ended up in the care of Pharaoh's daughter. He said he could not do the job because he could not speak. So, Moses went in to Pharaoh armed with his brother to speak for him and said, "Let my people go!" Xuan, when he arrived at the scene of the battle, calmly told the king, "Send your people home, they will be killed. I can take care of this myself." In moments the sea turned red with blood, as Xuan hurled his lightening bolts. Moses was there, in Egypt, for the plague in which the rivers turned to blood.

After their liberation, with Moses as the leader, the entire nation of Israel is left to wander in the wilderness 40 years until they gained a sense of unity and until the last memory of oppression was extinguished. After physical liberation became a reality, with a nation of externally dependent and complaining people on his hands, Moses chose to go to the mountain and talk directly to God, who gave him the tablets of the law. The law served to provide an external force, a stringent moral basis for the ethnic separation and identification which was in progress.

All of these heroes countered the discourse of repression with a discourse of resistance. Moses, Judith and Xuan were able, because of their *marginalization*, to tap into the pyrotechnics of *real* magical realism. They are subversive because they dealt in rational ways with irrational things. In the hierarchical church, spiritual/physical problems can be handled in supernatural ways. But consistent with the cultural history of her people, for Rigoberta Menchú the gods invest their power in their *least* because they are not encumbered with the process of the real/rational world. It is possible to do something about one's life if one is willing to take responsibility. People who have been without power, who are not part of the rational world, subvert the hierarchical system in religion, politics and life, thus freeing themselves to produce. The idea of praxis is revolutionary. Rigoberta maintains practical applications of praxis:

> We believe that the Bible is a necessary weapon for our people. *Today I can say that it is a struggle which cannot be stopped.* Neither governments nor imperialism can stop it because it is a struggle of hunger and poverty. Neither the government or imperialism can say, "Don't be hungry." We are all dying of hunger. It's not the document that brings the change, it is more that each one of us learns to understand his reality and wants to devote himself to others. (Menchú 1984: 135)

After Rigoberta Menchú understood the oppressive system that is inherent in Catholic Action, she further reflected on the conflict between the church and her idea of reality. What Rigoberta Menchú sees are the things that are *not*. Those things refer to her and to her life. She is literally *other*, what is not included, invisible. Her reaction is to reconfigure the idea of *other*. By discontinuing all the stances and postures that have to do with her relation to others and her marginality, and concentrating on her *self* and her preference, she dislocates the traditional configuration of core/periphery and privileges her own position. She accommodates her spiritual exile. Her work is at the border between visibility and invisibility, between silence and articulation. Just because there are borders (i.e. limits and extremities) does not mean they are menial or peripheral. These borders are the intersections of creative consciousness, aesthetic experience, growth and interconnection. They are not a sign of a schizophrenic split of loyalties between two identities. They signify resolution and reconciliation.

Referring back to the Intertext, we reread Bakhtin's assessment of the *here and now world*:

> Amid the good things of this here and now world are also to be found false connections that distort the authentic nature of things, false associations established and reinforced by tradition and sanctioned by religious and official ideology. Objects and ideas are united by false hierarchical relationships inimical to their nature. These false links are incorporated by scholastic thought and by a false theological casuistry shot through with centuries of error. It is necessary to destroy and rebuild this false picture of the world. It is necessary to liberate these objects and permit them to enter into the free unions that are organic to them no matter how monstrous these unions might seem. On the

basis of this new matrix of objects, a new picture of the world necessarily opens up—a world permeated with an internal and authentic necessity. (Bakhtin 1981: 169)

One of these seemingly monstrous unions is the reconciliation between charity/love and violence. The story of Judith "made us think that a people could not be victorious with out a just war. There is a church of the poor which is at war. We opted for the just war" (Menchú 1984: 132). The Christian hierarchy is not able to join the people's struggle; this means that it will disappear in Guatemala. We understand from Bakhtin and Rigoberta Menchú and from the ideas of liberation theology that the impetus for the development of the idea of liberation is an ethical sensitivity and commitment, implying that we be led not to social commentary but to action. We will be led to decry and resolve the conflicts in unjust social relations, called *sinful acts* by Gutiérrez in his *Theology of Liberation*. Bakhtin tells us that love is a creative, generative form of attention, and time-giving, which sustains change and productive energy. Further, Bakhtin writes that in aesthetic acts a person is *good* because we love him. We do not *love* a person because he is good. The constitution of the aesthetic experience is an act of love, a true revolutionary action, a mediation between the cognitive and the ethical in a work or a being proper.

Gutiérrez writes that in the context of class struggle today, "To love one's enemies presupposes recognizing and accepting that one has class enemies and that it is necessary to combat them." The true act of love is the liberation of the oppressor from his belief that he can oppress. To be committed to peace and to recognize violence and its source (whether it be oppression or liberation) is to be able to act.[66]

> My father said that a man's head wasn't just for wearing a hat, but was for thinking about what the community should do to try and change things, and for that change to bring about change in society at every level. We wanted change so that we could express our feelings, and conduct our ceremonies again the way we used to. (Menchú 1984: 155)

Bakhtin clarifies, "One should remember that to live from within *myself*, from my own unique place in *being* does not mean at all that I live only for my own sake. For it is only from my own place that self-sacrifice is possible, that is, the answerable centrality of myself can be a *self-sacrificing* centrality" (Bakhtin 1993: 59). The more one proceeds toward individuation, the more it is possible to become comfortable with one's actual self. The more self-authorship develops, the more a manifest single and unique *self* becomes apparent. If we look at the traditional Western conception of self-denial, iterated in the lives of the martyrs, whose onus is pathetic and unctuous self-abasement, and reconfigure it within the context of the developing self and its interdependence with the world around it, we begin to see the new archetype emerging. The emphasis is quite different. The offering and service that emanate from this processual development come from freedom, not from a need for propitiation or from a shortcoming. This new ethical identity is by nature giving, not needy. It is characterized by understanding, a consciousness that a selfless act itself is part of an integrated process. In fact, choosing to become is an act of service, which includes immediate and future completeness, as well as an enriched collective consciousness. When we understand this construction, it is possible to see why Judith, Xuan and Rigoberta Menchú would be willing to die for their beliefs.[67]

Reconciliation with *Ladinos*: Reconciliation with Language

Rigoberta Menchú is pushing at the boundaries of her life. She has assessed the opinions of outsiders, her history and culture and religion. She has unified her thinking. What is left is for her to leave consideration of the world as she knows it and to assess the outside world as it relates to her objective: the liberation of her people.

The animosity toward the *Ladino*, or outside world, which characterizes the thinking of Rigoberta Menchú until this juncture in her development, has been based on several factors. First, she has learned about the Conquest and its effects on the culture and life of her people, through oral history. She does have a critical consciousness and a sense of place with which to assess the outside world. Her experience has showed her that *Ladinos* are not trustworthy. She uses as examples her father's politicization while in jail, her personal experience as a maid in the city, the nuns who wouldn't answer her questions, as well as the relationship with the land owners and the INTA, who usurped her family land. "What I cannot forgive, and this is something which has contributed to my hate for these people, is that they said they came to help us," she laments (Menchú 1984: 104). This is not casual prejudice based on hearsay. Her experiences have been completely negative. Her opinion is justified. She understands who wields power.

When Rigoberta becomes critical of the values and mythology of non-Catholic *Ladino* culture, she wonders, "What does a *Ladino* have that I don't? Are some parts of his body different?" (Menchú 1984: 168). She understands that the *Ladino* has many ways of making his voice heard: He can read, write and speak a metropolitan language and can be understood by a majority of people in Guatemala. "Something I want to tell you," writes Rigoberta Menchú, "is that I had a friend. He was the man who taught me Spanish. He was a *Ladino*. . . . That *compañero* taught me many things, one of which was that some of my ideas were wrong, like saying that all *Ladinos* were bad. He didn't teach me with words, but by the way he behaved towards me" (Menchú 1984: 165).

Later, Rigoberta describes her political group as a mix of *Ladinos* and *indígenas*. She saw for the first time that oppression was not limited to indigenous people; that some *Ladinos* were also poor. The emphasis that is placed on her emotional revolution toward "the good *compañero*," as she calls him, shows that her discussions and debates at that time were seminal in her thinking and in her willingness in the future to speak with *Ladinos*. In another place she writes that she had difficulty turning around and criticizing a *Ladino* because their cultural mores are different. "I was raised to be obedient" (Menchú 1984: 98). She writes that when she was young, she was incapable of disobedience. At first, she had trouble being aggressive. She writes that she began to understand that she knew certain things that others did not, and that she had to stand up for her opinions, even if it meant that she had to tell a *Ladino* that he was wrong. "Discrimination had made me isolate myself completely from the world of our *compañeros ladinos*. . . . As I said, I am an Indianist, an Indianist down to my fingertips. But I didn't understand this in the proper way, because we can only understand when we start talking to each other" (Menchú 1984: 166). Menchú overcomes her training to be obedient, her conditioning toward feeling inferior and her unilateral hatred of *Ladinos* to do so.

It became clear to her that while *Ladinos* had many ways of making their voices heard, she would have none if she did not speak for herself. Her critical reflection and reassessment of her situation allowed her to understand what Bakhtin writes, "The other is intimately associated with the world. *I am located on the tangent, as it were, to a given state of affairs*" (Bakhtin 1990: 40). She realized what it means to be marginal in the dominant discourse, to exist peripherally, at the borders of another person's reality. "So I learned many things with the *Ladinos*, but most of all to understand our problem and the fact that we had to solve it ourselves" (Menchú 1984: 167). In other words, she needed to take responsibility for her *self*. Rigoberta's philosophy is very pragmatic. She uses available tools whether she is teaching, learning to make booby-traps or learning to speak. Menchú discovered that her oppressors had given her the tool—Spanish—with which to organize. She begins to understand the need to adopt the speech of the *Ladino* for political reasons. She writes, "I will speak Spanish so that we don't need inter-mediaries" (Menchú 1984: 110). She would mediate herself. This action demonstrates the function of *another other*.

Rigoberta states, "Siempre han dicho: Pobres indios que no saben hablar. Entonces muchos hablan por ellos; por eso me decidí a aprender el Castellano" [They have always said: Poor Indians who don't know how to speak. A lot of people speak for them; that is why I decided to learn to speak Spanish]. Even after she developed a sense of the spectrum of difference contained within the *other*, and she decided to learn to speak Spanish as the common language to help her relationships, she faced still another problem. As she traveled to different areas and slept in the houses of different *compañeros*, she was distressed to discover that they could not understand one another. She began to understand that even within *sameness* there is *otherness*.

> I asked myself: How is this possible? What an effective barrier this has been. But I began learning Cakchiquil and Tzuithil. I began to wonder if it wasn't better to learn first one and then another. Since Spanish was the language that united us, why learn all the twenty-two other languages in Guatemala? (Menchú 1984: 162)

Menchú realized that the dialect, their one non-*Ladino* trait and the exclusive provenience of her people, could be used as a method of exclusion. By encouraging the dialects and not the common language, those in power had prevented Mayan amalgamation. So, Rigoberta Menchú emphasized, "I learned to speak Spanish out of necessity" (Menchú 1984: 162).

Metamorphosis

Metamorphosis begins with a conscious volition to change. Making metamorphosis a separate category also reflects intent. Metamorphosis is not a debut so much as it is a process of recognition and transformation that may indicate a sudden change in consciousness. Without prepara-tion, the opportunity for transformation or the *deus ex machina* would not be perceived as a fortuitous circumstance, as a useful opportunity. In the introduction we described how it was possible to absorb negative outside influences and remain "drenched in muteness and invisibility." We showed how at a minimal level of consciousness an individual could recognize oppression and reconcile himself to it without any self-differentiation, thereby aborting the process of self-individuation.

While Bakhtin does not write about metamorphosis in this way, he does write strongly and continuously about coming to a place of accepting ethical responsibility and understanding. He writes about an essential moment when there was a unitary existence between the actually performed act and its answerability. This answerability of an actually performed act is the taking into account all of the factors, a taking into account of the *sense* validity as well as its factual performance in all its concrete historicity and individuality. "This answerability knows a unitary place, a unitary context in which the action has theoretical validity." Functional and theoretical discourse are untied here in praxis. "An answerable act constitutes a going out once and for all from within possibility into what is once occurrent. There is no reason to worry about whether this act is in and of itself irrational—it is undivided wholeness and therefore more than rational, it is answerable. This is a first philosophy" (Bakhtin 1993: 35-36).

Menchú writes that she was disturbed, ashamed at her confusion about life. She was a grown woman, at least in her community's eyes. She was about twenty years old. About her community she states:

> [My community's] ideas were very pure because they had never been outside their community. *We'd* been down to the *fincas*, but *they* hadn't known anything different. Going to the capital in a lorry brings about a change in an Indian, which he suffers inside himself. (Menchú 1984: 121)
>
> I *went through a painful change within myself.* What did exploitation mean to me? Why do they reject us? Why is the Indian not accepted? Why was it that the land used to belong to us? Why don't outsiders accept Indian ways? What happens if we rise up against the rich? Catholic Action submitted us to tremendous oppression. The moment I learned to identify my enemies was very important to me. (Menchú 1984: 123)

To describe the process of metamorphosis occurring within Menchú, we can rely on Bakhtin, who explains, "Understanding is impossible without evaluation. The person who understands must not reject the possibility of changing or even abandoning his already prepared viewpoints and positions. In the act of understanding, a struggle occurs that results in mutual change and enrichment" (Bakhtin, 1986: 142).

I told our community that our situation had nothing to do with fate but was something which was imposed on us. We have to defend ourselves against it—defend our parents rights. I didn't sleep much thinking about the future. *These weren't empty dreams; they were dreams coming true.* (Menchú 1984: 120)

The second time they caught a soldier, Rigoberta Menchú writes, rather than explaining their position, and asking for help, as they had with the first captive, they questioned him and found out about how they treated the soldiers in the army. This is a quantum change. At first, they reached out to a soldier to explain their position, hoping the other would see. In the second instance, they reached out to him to get information that they needed to understand their own situation for themselves. We see that the focus and the impetus of the actions have changed from external dependence to self-reflection and personal responsibility.

The Growth of a Modulated, Self-Sustaining Person

Because of her process of self-authorship, Rigoberta Menchú is, according to Bakhtin's theories, the "one who is thinking theoretically, contemplating aesthetically, and acting ethically. This is the way in which a living consciousness becomes a cultural consciousness, and a cultural consciousness becomes embodied in a living consciousness" (Bakhtin 1993: 33, 43). Menchú writes:

I was by now an educated woman—not in the sense of any schooling and even less in the sense of being well-read. But I knew the history of my people and the history of my *compañeros* from other ethnic groups. This taught me that even though a person may learn to read and write, he should not accept the false education they give our people. Our people must not think as the authorities think. They must not let others think for them. We can select what is truly relevant for our people. Our lives show us what this is. It has guaranteed our existence. (Menchú 1984: 170)

Rigoberta paid a price for her decision to go on with the struggle. She writes that she was always afraid, wanted to be dead, got ulcers and was tired of living. Later she writes that she was not afraid anymore because she was not thinking. "When you are in danger and you know you've only a minute of your life left, you don't remember what you did yesterday" (Menchú 1984: 238). In his reflections on the last moments in the village Víctor Montejo writes, "I became familiar with what a man thinks of at his last moments when he is scared out of his wits—nothing" (Montejo 1987: 57).

To get the clearest picture, we must view developments in the life of Rigoberta Menchú as outside observers rather than through the record she gives of her process of interior growth. How did outside circumstances affect her internal development? Her situation is unique. It is impossible to think that Rigoberta as an individual could have been the same without all the special things that happened to her. She traveled and spoke when she was young. She identified highly with her father over her mother. She had generational continuity. Her mother's father was still living at 106—a miracle in a country where the age at death for an indigenous individual is frequently less than 50 years. Rigoberta writes that when a person lives, he can have a life expectancy of 60 years (Menchú 1984: 145).

Throughout her life, Menchú has shrugged traditional role models. She comments, "The community is very suspicious of a woman like me who is twenty-three and they don't know where I've been or where I've lived" (Menchú 1984: 61). She lost the confidence of the community and contact with her neighbors, who were meant to be looking after her all the time. She decided not to have children and marry. She decided to learn Spanish and become educated. Finally, because of her political initiatives, she was expelled from her homeland. Her mother encouraged her to be *different* while maintaining her sense of her origins and duties. As a child, she first complained to her mother that she wished she were dead:

> "Mother, I don't want to live. Why didn't I die when I was little? How can we go on living?" I had a lot of ideas but knew I couldn't express them all. I wanted to read or speak or write Spanish. I told my father this. He said, "Who will teach you? I know of no schools and I have no money for them anyway." My father didn't agree with my idea because I was trying to leave the community to go far away and find what was best for me. He said, "You'll forget about your common heritage. If you leave, it will be for good. If you leave the community, I will not support you."
>
> But I responded, "I want to learn." I kept on and on. (Menchú 1984: 89)

Although we find out that her father changed his mind, we also understand that the community was very suspicious of a woman who was out in the world. In fact, Rigoberta writes that it was her father who took her around and taught her how to speak in public when she was a child (Menchú 1984: 190, 194). The eyes of the whole community were on her. It was important that she set a good example as a woman. On the other hand, Rigoberta writes that her mother was not able to express herself politically, but was politicized through her work and thought that

We should learn to be women, but women who were useful to the community. From when we were very small we went with her and had to learn from her example and copy the little things she taught us about politics. My mother was very courageous. My mother made no distinction between the men's struggle and the women's struggle. She said I don't want to make you stop feeling a woman, but your participation in the struggle must be equal to that of your brothers." (Menchú 1984: 219)

In spite of the role model provided by her mother, Rigoberta's writing suggests that she sided with her father more than her mother. She quotes her father:

My father told me, "Learning is difficult, but you do it and you learn." When he had meetings with people, he'd choose me first so I'd stop keeping my opinions to myself. I didn't like intruding when all the others were giving their views. So my father taught me how to speak. I hardly ever fought with any of the boys in my village, because I've got more or less the same attitudes as they have. (Menchú 1984: 194)

Her mother encouraged her to be different while maintaining her sense of her origins and duties. As the conflicts and persecution progressed, Rigoberta's father told his daughters that they could do as they wish:

To be independent, give everything to the struggle without anyone behind us ordering us about or forcing us to do anything. He gave us total freedom, but would like us to use that freedom for the good of the people to teach people what he had taught us. (Menchú 1984: 155)

We read that her father developed his hatred for his enemies while in jail, when he also began to be discriminate as to who the enemy would be. Her father's understanding and defense against oppression pushed him into the world. Rigoberta is influenced by the same dynamics.

Projection of the Self into the World at Large

In Guatemala, there are no stars among the poor.
Rigoberta Menchú

The impelling inspiration of my small life and the boundless world
is that of my participative non-alibi in being.
It is only from this small compellently actual world
that expansion may proceed.
M.M. Bakhtin

The drama between the metaphysical/spiritual world and the public world has reached its denouement. Rigoberta Menchú leaves her own village and travels to other villages to teach. She reminds us that, until that point, her village had been safe from kidnapping and rapes. In other hamlets she instructs residents in what she has taught successfully in her own village: public safety and the nature of the indigenous oppression. Her father has released her from family obligation, allowing her to be independent and moving about wherever she wanted, to help. Her dream, in this second organizing experience, was to go on fighting and getting to know the people more closely. What transpires thereafter is the result of her reflective commitment as a conscious being. Her position, now, is similar to that of Víctor Montejo when he defended the village. Rigoberta Menchú's position parallels Bakhtin's observation that the answerable centrality of the self is the only place from which an act of self-sacrifice can be made. "Living from my own unique place in Being, does not mean that I live for my own sake" (Bakhtin 1993: 59). This *non alibi in being*, as Bakhtin called it, is constituent of the self-defined individual. Literally that individual is no longer defined by her need to respond to the external stimulation of others in her surroundings, their demands and expectations. The need for excuses, envy, guilt or shame has been eliminated because those traits define the individual by deficiency. Rather, Menchú's development and action are a direct result of her critical reflection on her reality, a position which is internally and self-generated, although sentient and responsive to the external world.

> My father said, "Where you are going you may not have control over your life. You can be killed at any time. You could be killed tomorrow." But I knew that teaching others how to defend themselves against the enemy was a commitment I had to make-a commitment to my people

and my commitment as a Christian. I have faith and I believe that happiness belongs to everyone, but that happiness has been stolen by a few. (Menchú 1984: 141)

Rigoberta Menchú recaps for us the activity of her other family members. Her mother is also organizing. It was the women in the towns who took over the mayors' offices, to "demonstrate their revulsion." The women, who understood that the men would be kidnapped and tortured, wanted to see if the military was so shameless that they would also massacre women and children.

The story line of *Me llamo Rigoberta Menchú* becomes succinct and direct beginning with 1979, and the 16 days when her brother was tortured. It develops a staccato of urgency, moving as it does from sentient historicity to news-bite chronology. The emotional tone changes. On September 23, 1979, the Menchú family heard that the military was surrounding a town called Chajul, and that her brother was there. The family walked over the mountains for two days. When they arrived at the town they found 500 soldiers. They were stopped and interrogated more than twenty times. They were allowed access to the town because they said they were going to visit the saint of that town, but also because they ignored the prohibitions of the military police. The soldiers were waiting for the men of the village to return. Again, this situation is similar to the one which opens Montejo's *Death of a Guatemalan Village.*

The family entered the village as two lorries of the military brought the torture victims into the plaza. The family saw the victims burned. We recorded that Rigoberta saw them and *how* she saw them in an earlier section of this study. Her brother was 16 years old when he died, the first member of the Menchú family to be tortured and killed.

Exactly at that moment, Rigoberta writes, this savage action turned the tide of her life. She queries, "If it is a sin to kill a human being, how can what this regime is doing not be a sin?" (Menchú 1984: 176). At this juncture the philosophical ethical and moral considerations of her life coalesce with her active faith. She reframes her initial questions, "How or why did they do this to me, and what have I done to deserve this?" Reframing the question allows her to transcend constructions of mimesis/alterity, self/other, which bind the imagination. Her transcendence allows her to continue defending her faith, keeping it within the revolutionary process.

Again she recaps that both she and her mother decide to continue organizing actively to protect other families from "the horror film of her brother's death." Her mother, half dead with grief because of her brother's burning, decided to join the insurgency. " 'I may be old but I'm joining the guerrillas. I shall avenge my son with arms.' Sometimes my mother was mad. 'No crying! Fighting is what we want,' she would say" (Menchú 1984: 176).

A new phase began in Menchú's life when she obtained an interdependent system of support from the peasant organization, CUC, and her father, Vicente Menchú left to become part of the revolutionary movement. Rigoberta did not see her father alive again except for a brief period in November 1979 in El Quiché. At this time her father told her to be in Guatemala City for an action against the government. Rigoberta writes that the hamlet in which she was working was in danger, and the group she was helping did not want her to leave. Therefore, she remained behind in the village, rather than going to the capital to see her father.

The march on the capital, and the occupation of the Spanish embassy January 31, 1980—both organized by her father—pointed out to her another problem with poverty; it limited her exposure to the tactics of those in power. She writes that she thought that the government would give those who occupied the embassy, including her father, permission to leave the country. Instead, the building was set on fire. Bodies were turned to ashes. At first, Rigoberta thought that her entire remaining family was in the embassy.

> I had to face some terrible moments. First when the news came that the bodies were unrecognizable and I thought that my mother and brothers were there. What I could not bear was the idea of them all dying together. We must all give our lives, I know, but not all together. Let there be one time when someone is left. I couldn't bear it. I wanted to die. (Menchú 1984: 176)

Bothered, Rigoberta writes that it was not just her father's death, but the knowledge that those who occupied the embassy were not ambitious for power. The protesters were only asking for enough to live on, to meet their people's needs. In the optimism of her faith and because of the lack of experience, she misjudged the feral nature of her opposition. Rigoberta writes that all the peasants knew that the people who occupied the embassy had no fire arms, only machetes. Yet, her father was found, after the burning, with five bullet holes in his head and one in his heart. He was stiff. No one knows what really happened there. Was it a sulfur bomb that left the corpse so stiff? Rigoberta Menchú is unwilling to make something up from her imagination. The event remains shrouded in mystery. Her father's murder elevated him to the status of hero of the resistance.

Rigoberta discovers yet another occlusion in her world view: the absence of global thinking—a weakness in the internal peasant organization. The peasants were too poor and inexperienced to understand that exposure in the international press and visibility when speaking about the problems in Guatemala would bring international celebration of their cause. In fact, Rigoberta appeared oblivious to the unstable traveling conditions throughout Guatemala. She adds that she still did not know what was the most effective-to continue to go around to different communities to raise consciousness or take up arms. Her decision to work with the peasants organizing committee, PUC, fostered continuity.

As a clarification of her decision not to marry, she writes of being in love and then choosing to be alone—a decision she made for herself:

> The time came when I saw clearly, actually when I became a revolutionary, that I was fighting for a people and for many children who hadn't had anything to eat. I could see how sad it would be for a revolutionary not to leave a seed, because that seed, left behind would see the fruit of her work. But I saw that it would be easier for me to die if I weren't leaving anyone behind to suffer. All this horrified me, and gave me a lot to think about. (Menchú 1984: 176)

Events that followed indeed gave Menchú much to think about. In February 1980, a strike occurred involving agricultural workers—80,000 sugar and cotton workers in the south of the country and the coastal strip where the plantations are. Peasants, who were paid only for one ton per load, sabotaged cotton-picking machines that picked in excess of one ton per load. On April 19, 1980, Rigoberta's mother is kidnapped, tortured, raped and left for dead underneath a tree, guarded by soldiers until the bones were picked clean by vultures.

Menchú is forced into hiding in the capital. She sees her twelve-year-old sister, also organizing guerrilla movements. Her little sister tells Rigoberta, "What has happened to us is a sign of victory. It gives us a reason for fighting. We must behave like revolutionary women" (Menchú 1984: 176). Menchú moves to the home of some supporters in Huehuetenango where she becomes ill with ulcers. She reports that in a dream, her father tells her to get on with her life. Rigoberta then reflects that if she is going to die it should be for a cause, not just for herself. Soon thereafter, she is spotted by the military on the street and forced to hide kneeling at the altar rail in a church, while the soldiers pass at her back, exiting into the market place. Rigoberta Menchú writes that there was a moment in her life when she just did not want to hide anymore. "I was fed up and tired of hiding in houses. I knew it meant for me that I would be kidnapped or killed. I felt that I didn't want to die, that I had a lot of things to do that it wasn't time for me to die yet" (Menchú 1984: 176). After assessing the alternatives she writes, "This is my cause. No one can take my faith" (Menchú 1984: 176). Although she remained committed to a political life, Rigoberta was marginalized everywhere. Now thrice dispossessed. First from her family land, again from her culture and her people, on the *finca* and in the city and now from her own country, she is ejected into the world, into a metropolitan existence as an exile in Mexico City. She writes that she could not believe that she would be forced to abandon her country. She returned to Guatemala clandestinely, to continue organizing "after their furious urge to capture us had calmed down."

In other sectors, Sololá and Xelá, the military was bombing, and taking captives for the army. There were now four political organizations working and there was a need for another coalition. In January 1981, a coalition was formed with the following groups: The Ejército Guerrillero de los Pobres(EGP); the Organización del Pueblo en Armas (OPRA); the Fuerzas Armadas Rebeldes (FAR); and the Partido Guatemalteco del Trabajo(PGT). This was the nucleus of the leadership. This united front called itself the January 31 Popular Front. It included the Revolutionary Workers Groups, the coordinating committee in the shanty towns; the Vicente Menchú Revolutionary Christians; the Robin García Secondary Students Revolutionary Front; and the Robin García University Students Front. The first coalition between students and peasants had been at the burning of the Spanish Embassy where Vicente Menchú died.

In May 1981, there was a demonstration with barricades and propaganda bombs and lightening meetings in the capital, resulting in a one-day government shutdown. In July 1981, the government sent all priests a telegram. "The ecclesiastical hierarchy is driving around with bodyguards," writes Menchú, parenthetically. Archbishop Casariegos blessed the electoral campaign. All priests were required to give their names and addresses and have their pictures taken. Lucas, the President of Guatemala, called on them to initiate a literacy campaign. Only a few nuns responded that they had been teaching literacy for a long time. Everyone else was silent, fearing for their lives.

Rigoberta Menchú continued to organize, traveling throughout Mexico. She heard that her youngest sister, at eight years of age, had joined the guerrillas. While in Mexico, she met Europeans who had helped and known her parents. The Anglos from Europe encouraged her to take her sisters to Europe where they could get an education and alleviate their suffering. However, she and her sisters chose to return to Guatemala. Menchú then worked with the Vicente Menchú Revolutionary Christians, whose job it was to denounce the inequities of the church and "put into practice what a being a Christian means" (Menchú 1984: 176). She writes that she tried to explain to others why faith was more important to her than Marxism alone. Her calling, she explained, is to defend her people and their faith from within the revolutionary process.

In January 1982, she was invited to visit Paris as a representative of the January 31 Popular Front. She meets Elizabeth Burgos-Debray and the story of her life is repeated as her testimonial. Her past is now her prologue.

Exile

Exile and the literature it produces represent and express a special type of solitude that cannot be endured without adequate self-definition. The life of Rigoberta Menchú and the testimonial that she wrote are not separate entities. *Me llamo Rigoberta Menchú y asi nació mi conciencia* is a reflection on and production of her growth and understanding. She became a heroine in her own life because she placed her life as a lived process in print for consummation by the eyes of others. Bakhtin writes in *Speech Genres and Other Essays*, that "in the event in the life of a text, its true essence develops on the boundary between two subjects, two consciousnesses." The testimonial is a special speech genre, in which the "whole utterance is made in anticipation of a response" (Bakhtin 1986: 170, 176).

Rigoberta Menchú has become what Bakhtin calls in *Toward a Philosophy of the Act*, "a participative, incarnated consciousness, who does not see culture as a self-contained consciousness" (Bakhtin 1993: 176). Her word/testimonial is an act which she performs and that act, Bakhtin states, is alive only in the unitary and unique event of her being. As author, she is the "uniquely active form giving energy that is manifested not in psychologically conceived consciousness but in a durable and valuable cultural product" (Bakhtin 1993: 176). She writes of herself:

> I was a grown-up woman, a woman who could face this situation. I told myself, "Rigoberta, you are just going to have to grow up a little bit more." Of course my experience has been very painful; but I thought about a lot of things, especially all the other orphaned children who couldn't speak and tell their story as I could. I tried to forget so many things but at the same time I had to face up to them as a woman with a certain level of consciousness. (Menchú 1984: 224-25)

In her testimonial, Menchú makes a space for herself and her people outside of the externally oppressive system in which she grew up. In doing so she became a special type of outsider. Not just three times displaced; not only as a woman in exile; but as a special and unique category of reflective individual. Her personal development lead to a new sense of *other*ness. She is intact in the transcendent sphere I have called *another other*. Bakhtin in his last work, translated in *Speech Genres and other Essays*, writes about the inexhaustibility of the second consciousness, which is the consciousness of the person who understands and responds:

> Herein lies a potential infinity of responses, languages and codes. Infinity against infinity. The *supra person*, witness and the judge of the whole human being, of the whole *I* and consequently someone who is no longer the person, no longer the *I* but the *other*. (Bakhtin 1986: 137)

Paul de Man writes of Bakhtin that all his literary characters carry within themselves the image of their oppressors.[68] We must also carry within ourselves the images of our liberation, if we are to become the heroines of our own lives, through reconciliation, self-fulfillment, and the authorship of the *self*.

Conclusion

This study has shown how the authorship of the self proceeds from a stage of (aphonic) muteness and unquestioning invisibility through a metamorphosis into a new and developing ethical consciousness. This authorship of the self parallels the principal stages that M.M. Bakhtin described in the development of the novel. It also parallels in many key ways the hermeneutical process described by Gutiérrez in his *Theology of Liberation*, and by Paulo Freire in his process of consciousness formation. It is a hermeneutics of interpretation and explanation. In both Menchú and Bakhtin we can see the immediate result of this process as *lived life* and also as life hoped for, a discourse distinguished by the ethically responsible *now*.

I have chosen to call this fully developed interactive individual *another other*. This individual is self-defined, ethical, aware of and committed to roots and available to others. She can see another as that other sees himself, without diminution of personhood of either herself or the *other*. Bakhtin intimated in his writing that this individual existed: a *supra I*, an individual with two consciousnesses, who can reflect clearly on himself and others, with necessary, concomitant objectification and understanding.

The *self-authored* individual is not diminished by reflection in another's eye nor is she diminished by her appropriation by outsiders. In fact, refraction through another's gaze increases both degree and level of interanimation. Rigoberta Menchú's present status also can be described as post-modern iconographic, a secular saint whose consciousness contains mythical, political and spiritual reality.

In traditional rhetoric when one is appropriated one becomes the object of someone else's discourse changing the individual subject from actor to shadow. This is, in essence, a loss of one's spiritual being. As Bakhtin has stated:

> To express oneself is to make oneself an object for another and for oneself. We can also reflect our attitude toward ourselves as objects. In this case our own discourse becomes an object and acquires a second, its own voice. But this second voice no longer casts a shadow, for it expresses pure relationship. (Bakhtin 1986: 110)

This text has shown that an investigation into the question, "How did we come to be in this place?" uncovers the inherent contradictions in the content of present cultural and social structures. This uncovering of contradictions is the root of a new type of consciousness.

Specifically, this work values both a sentient historicity and a spiritual ethnography as ways of explaining and dealing with the multiple manifestations of other states of being, a new spatial sphere of historical existence. At stake here is the questioning interpretation and validation of how we interpret our history, and which cultural developments we privilege. This study values the development of personal ethical consciousness and its effect on our view of history. Because a spiritual ethnography includes the issue of faith and therefore hope, although not necessarily of religion, it is a narrative structure not limited to or by experienced physical existence. This expansion is crucial because in the case of those who are oppressed, physical reality is often the experience of active, institutionalized, numbing violence.

This study has shown how writing one's life is a counter-discursive strategy for victims of violence, most especially women and those who have undergone systematic destruction of their cultural capital by externally imposed forces. The process described, both of self-authorship and the production of the testimonial are not processes for recounting pain, which someone else can live vicariously. The subject/writer retains her commentary. In both the spiritual ethnography and the testimonial exists an undisputed authorial presence that permeates the entire text. Holding on to one's own story prevents diminution or appropriation, except on one's own terms. Further, an interdependent-independent *self* is a relief from the sameness of the putative center. Going further, we can say that the social construction of Rigoberta Menchú and M.M. Bakhtin is synchronous with the concepts of fractal physics, a particle theory in which a variety of fluid configurations and responses exist, the locations of which are not predictable with any range of accuracy.[69] However, it is reflection and ethical responsibility in both Bakhtin and Menchú that produce a desire for the hermeneutic process which prevents systemic disintegration. An effective dislocation of the possible configuration of core/periphery occurs in development of self-authored individuals because they are free to discuss and decide on questions about themselves in inventive ways, outside the confines of traditional border work allotted to marginalized *others*. In Bakhtin, the only growth occurs at the borders, literally when we are outside ourselves. So, this process is a resolution of the social schizophrenia experienced by the fragmented, polarized or externally dependent *self*.

In Bakhtin, border disputes are indicative of areas not of contestation or marginalization but of growth into what he calls *benevolent demarcation*. Border writing as discussed by current writers often uses a traditional past to validate an uncertain future. Borders need not have peripheralized or marginalized connotations. They are interactive junctures for aesthetic production. Bakhtin, whose work, *Towards a Philosophy of the Act,* predates the aforementioned works by 50 years, explains that any text is an expression of consciousness, something which reflects the immediate condition and place of the author. Both writing and *being* are forms of textuality that convert images into symbols giving them both semantic depth and perspective. As a culture passes from oral tradition to written textuality, the testimonial provides both a bridge between these two worlds and a vehicle for its communication and expression, which privileges those unable to write because of lack of skills or power in language. *Me llamo Rigoberta Menchú, El Kanil,* and *Testimony: Death of a Guatemalan Village* all contribute to the development of a canon of national literature for the Mayan people, which occurs in the formation of a national identity. This canon of literature is characterized by both individual author and collective consciousness.

This study has shown that among the indigenous people of Guatemala there exists and has existed in the oral tradition an archetypal hero who rather than becoming great as a result of an annunciation, does so as a product of choice, an ethical decision based on a willingness to die for one's beliefs or one's people. This willingness to give one's life is generated not so much from a sense of inadequacy, guilt or shame on the part of the individual, but as a result of an interdependent-independent system of self-definition. The final individual product is one who, as Bakhtin writes, "thinks theoretically, contemplates aesthetically and acts ethically."

The world of Rigoberta Menchú is a culture of complex societies. It affirms difference by not joining others solely on the basis of common oppression but uses that knowledge as a tool for change. Previous and current discourses have mythologized a homogeneity of background which has been discarded or questioned by post-modernist enthusiasm for the de-centered subject. However, postmodernism as a construction describes a cultural phenomenon formulated by non-subjects.

Rigoberta Menchú has dealt effectively with her status as a non-subject as well as with the erosion and reconfiguration of her traditional culture at the same time as those in Europe are dealing with theirs.

However, in both Bakhtin and Menchú we can see a transcendent sphere of individuality emerging, contingent on solidarity, not sameness or mimeses. Bakhtin writes in *Speech Genres and Other Essays* that:

> There exists a very strong and yet one-sided, and thus untrustworthy, idea that in order to better understand a foreign culture(other) one must enter into it and forget one's own, and view the world through the eyes of the other. This idea is one-sided. Creative understanding does not renounce itself, and it forgets nothing. Our real exterior can be seen and understood only by other people because they are located outside us in space and *because they are others.*" (Bakhtin 1986: 6)

In the view of Bakhtin and Montejo and Menchú, each of us is responsible for our world because we are the only ones in it. Doubting our values prevents adhesion to them, but we still remain personally responsible for our actions. Individual accountability is not an excuse for lack of group action. Group action is needed for consummation of this dynamic interaction. Because we are all responsible there is no blame, only an *other* to see us and to consummate the aesthetic experience of the *lived horizon of our being.*

Endnotes

[1] Mikhail Mikhailovich Bakhtin, *Speech Genres and Other Essays*, eds. Caryl Emerson and Michael Holquist, trans. Vern W. McGee (Austin: University of Texas Press, 1986), 142.

[2] *Me llamo Rigoberta Menchú* was originally published in French (Paris: Editions Gallimard and Elisabeth Burgos, 1983), and was translated into Spanish in the same year (Barcelona: Editorial Argos Vergara, S.A., 1983). While the original Spanish title translates as "My Name is Rigoberta Menchú, and This Is How My Consciousness Was Born," the English edition was renamed *I, Rigoberta Menchú: An Indian Woman in Guatemala*. Unless otherwise stated, the work of Rigoberta Menchú is quoted from the English edition (London: Verso, 1984).

[3] Traditional hermeneutics in scriptural terms was the use of the Bible as a unified interpreting tool for life. Gradually the process acknowledged that each person brings something with her to help in interpretation, so that the apportionment meaning is no longer solely the aegis of scripture.

In *Theology of Liberation* (New York: Orbis Books, 1988), xxx-xxxv, Gustavo Gutiérrez writes that in theology, faith comes first, then reflection/discourse about God and finally *praxis* (action) based on commitment and prayer, which produces and tempers the process. All of this is done within the context of culture.

For philosopher Hans-Georg Gadamer and for liberation theology in general, individuals are in constant conversation about the nature of things, critically interpreting texts and their everyday lives, not for their own selves alone but as part of a communal activity. The result of this process is praxis. Historical praxis is characterized by the manipulation of history and natural forces. Liberating praxis is a struggle to achieve clarity and equity through reassessment of the past and the development of critical consciousness of the possibilities inherent in an equitable future.

For me, the hermeneutical circle represents the struggle to reconcile everything that the five steps of this transformation entail. The real is not exhausted by the present, but looks to the future, not as wishing and optimism, but as hopeful expectation. This hermeneutic process represents a bridge between appearance and essence, which prods individuals to look forward, to continue to create themselves.

There are interesting parallels between Bakhtin's concept of "confessional self-accounting" and hermeneutics as I have described it. Bakhtin writes that outside God, outside of trust in absolute otherness, self-consciousness and self-utterance are impossible: "The moment of otherness is axiologically transcendent to self-consciousness and is in principle not guaranteed. Life from within itself is nothing else but the actualization of faith. That is, we need hope and faith, non-contentment and possibility" (Bakhtin 1993: 143-45).

Consummation of an act or thought requires another for its completeness. In this completeness there is also the infinite possibility of new growth and development within the context of interrelations among others. Here we see the interaction between what constitutes the future and what constitutes faith—the expression of hope—into the future. Completeness/consummation of an act and reconciliation is the end of an hermeneutical cycle. This is not a static product. When viewed from the outside, we see that it generates dialogical possibilities rather than termination. Nor is the hermeneutics of living solely a utopian project. We need to say that we are being liberated even as we speak and act, and that we look to further liberation and its sustenance.

For a thorough reference for the above see Rebecca Chopp, *The Praxis of Suffering* (New York: Orbis Books, 1986). Chopp in her introduction paraphrases Paul Tillich's definition of liberation theology: "To understand liberation theology, we must grasp one basic claim, suffering and its quest for freedom is the fundamental reality of human experience as well as the location of God, Christ and the church in history. Liberation theology urges action, strategy and a change in human existence; it demands justice, equality and freedom in Christian witness. Consequently, liberation theology is a new language of God, seeking, in the present historical situation, to be the voice of those who suffer" (Chopp 1986: 3).

I would like to mention here that inasmuch as constructions of philosophy themselves are constrained by ideology, the issues of consciousness, rescue and revolution are problematized by the assumptions that surround them. Some of these considerations are taken up in the chapter, "Intertext". However, Roberto Rivera, in his forthcoming *The Oppositional Nature of Liberation Discourses*, describes this situation in detail. He writes, "The problem of borrowing those theories [Western ones] about the textual character of the social realm, communicative action and views about the Enlightenment is that since for the most part Third World theorists quote First World theorists out of context, there is always the possibility that these borrowings might interfere with the goals the Third World critics might have in mind" (Rivera 1995: 3). On page 200, he writes, "Both texts [that of Gutiérrez and that of Freire] reduce people to victims—in spite of their authors claim to the contrary—hence, reifying them. Both texts set out to accomplish the liberation of people and at the same time undermine this goal by promoting strategies that militate against people's autonomy. In the case of Gutiérrez, the discursive inconsistencies are less severe because he appropriates, unlike Freire, views that are most consistent with his enterprise."

It is in the light of these considerations that I propose the Bakhtinian model in this text.

[4]Paulo Friere, in *The Pedagogy of the Oppres* Publishing Co., 1985), 31, states, "The opp· image of the oppressor and adopted his gu¹ .. To surmount the situation of oppression its causes, so that through transforming actio. one that makes possible the pursuit of a fuller hu.

Seamus Deane, in *Nationalism Colonialism and Lin* University of Minnesota Press, 1990), writes, "In the atten₁, its *true* identity, a community often begins with the demolitio. stereotypes within which it has been entrapped. This is an intricate . since the stereotypes are successful precisely because they have been ₁. riorized. They are not merely impositions from the colonizer on the colonized. It is a matter of common knowledge that stereotypes are mutually generative of each other" (12).

[5]See Freire 1985: 33, "Liberation is thus a childbirth and a painful one. The man who emerges is a new man. . . . In order for the oppressed to be able to wage the struggle for liberation, they must perceive the reality of oppression not as a closed world from which there is no exit, but as a limiting situation which they can transform. This condition is a necessary but not a sufficient condition for liberation; it must be the motivating force for liberating action. Nor does the discovery by the oppressed that they exist in a dialectical relationship to the oppressor, as his antithesis—that without them, the oppressor could not exist—in itself constitute liberation."

Paolo Freire was a Brazilian educator who developed many of his ideas for literacy education from his association with Catholic Action at about the same time as Louis Althusser and Michel Foucault were involved with this singular segment of the community of the spirit in France. All, like Menchú, became disenchanted with it and moved on. Freire and M.M. Bakhtin share a common thread with the Russian developmental and cognitive psychologist, Lev Vgotsky, who wrote concurrently with Bakhtin, primarily in the 20s and 30s. Vgotsky's book, *Thought and Language*, was published in the United States by MIT Press in 1962. It appears from references that both were influenced throughout their careers by Vgotsky's work. One idea they share is that of inner speech, which with critical consciousness can produce a written text. The inability to relate one's personal perspective to a specific audience is a barrier to communication and, therefore, literacy. Oral communication offers clues to the audience response. Written communication requires an understanding of social and linguistic forms.

[6]See Gary Saul Morson and Caryl Emerson, *Rethinking Bakhtin* (Evanston, Illinois: Northwestern University Press, 1989).

[7]I privilege both forms equally. Although the form of a text is important, the primary concern of this paper is content and idea formation.

...tin, *Toward a Philosophy of the Act* (Austin: University of Texas
93).

akhtin, *The Dialogic Imagination*, ed. Michael Holquist, trans. Caryl
son and Michael Holquist (Austin: University of Texas Press, 1981).

s preface to *The Dialogic Imagination*, Michael Holquist says that "*novel*
the name Bakhtin gives to whatever force is at work within a given literary
system to reveal the limits, the artificial constraints of that system. Literary
systems are comprised of canons, and *novelization* is fundamentally anticanonical. It will not permit generic monologue. Always, it will insist on the
dialogue between what a given system will admit as literature and those texts
that are otherwise excluded from such a definition of literature. What is more
conventionally thought of as the novel is simply the most complex and
distilled expression of this impulse" (Bakhtin 1981: xxxii).

[11] Mary Louise Pratt, *Imperial Eyes* (London: Routledge, 1992).

[12] M.M. Bakhtin, *Art and Answerability*, eds. Michael Holquist, Vadim
Liapunov, trans. Vadim Liapunov (Austin: University of Texas Press, 1990),
6.

[13] Paul Ricoeur, in *Myself as Another*, trans. Kathleen Blamey (Chicago: University of Chicago Press, 1990), addresses a number of issues about narrative
and its functions, as the unfolding of identity that can only happen over time
and the interweaving of character development and plot which allow us to
see in depth, someone whose identity might be flattened in another discourse.
He focuses on ethical discourse as a function of human action. (I would say
"qualifier of human action" because it is *speaking* that makes us accountable
for our words.)

[14] John Beverley, "The Margin at the Center, Testimonial Narrative," *Modern Fiction Studies*, 1989, 35: 1, 13.

[15] Peter Hulme, *Colonial Encounters* (London: Chapman & Hall, 1987).

[16] Michel de Certeau, in the preface to *Heterologies, Discourse on the Other*
(1986), writes that the development of 'decolonialization' followed by a
period of 'reterritorialization' became rapidly conceptualized thorough notions of core and periphery. Former colonial peoples together with economically dominant nations constituted the core, whereas the former colonies
formed the periphery. Certeau states, "Part of the new economic crisis
certainly seems to have to do with the determination of such a new center.
Hegemonic tendencies of the cognitive realm is not the exclusive purview of
the traditional disciplines. It permeates the writings of even the most theoretically daring thinkers," 9-13.

[17] Sam Colop, *Ch'ob'anelab' Uk'aslemal Mayab' Amaq'*, cuaderno no. 1.
Guatemala, octubre 1991.

[18]Nora England, "Language and Ethnic Definition Among Guatemalan Mayans." Paper presented at American Anthropological Association, November 1988, states, "It is clear that the cultural content of Mayan identity can and does change quite radically without the destruction or even weakening of that identity."

[19]George Yudice and Franco Jean, *On Edge, The Crisis of Contemporary Latin American Culture* (University of Minnesota Press, 1989), 21.

[20]J. Jude Pansini "Ethnic Identity in Guatemala: The Impact of Current Events," undated paper, 1.

[21]*Anamnesis* is first seen in Plato's discussion of the rebirth of the *self* as a recreation of ancient ideas. In this century in psychoanalysis, it has been used to define the recall of an event, the action of which was completed in the past, and as a ritual designed to provoke action and response in the present. This interpretive act engenders a process of removing blocks from memory, correction of distortion, ordering of life events and the creating of a unified life story. Freud used the term to apply more to the emotional than the cognitive, more characterized by association than introspection. In some interpretive theories, psychosis is the result of a failure to connect or establish a credible link with one's past. In therapeutic situations silence is used by the patient, as a block to keep the past from being recalled.

[22]Víctor Montejo, working paper, undated, State University of New York at Stoneybrook.

[23]First Mayan Education Conference, "Síntesis de las tres ponencias presentadas por Wajshaquib Batz," Centro de Estudios de la Cultura Maya (CECMA) Sociedad el Adelanto.

[24]Nora England, "Language and Ethnic Definition Among Guatemalan Mayans," 1988, 18.

[25]Margarita López Raquec, "Implicaciones de la atomización linguistica en el idioma kaqchikel," Asociación Antropología Americana, noviembre 1991, Chicago.

[26]The first polemic in this tradition of reification was De Las Casas' in defense of the Indian in 1552. Another is the false charity described by Freire as the ego cloaked in false generosity *(Pedagogy of the Oppressed,* 39), as is Renato Rosaldo's concept of Imperialist Nostalgia, in which we kill the person and mourn the victim. Imperialist nostalgia is the reification of the remainder of a native trait by those who decimated it *(Culture and Truth).* In the Indigenist novels of Castellanos and Asturias *mestizaje* is the solution to the problem of Indian acculturation.

[27]Seamus Dean, *Nationalism, Colonialism and Literature* (Minneapolis, University of Minnesota Press, 1990), 8.

[28]Paulo Freire, *Pedagogy of the Oppressed*, 14.

[29]Owen Barfield, *Saving the Appearances, A Study in Idolatry* (Middletown, Conn.: Wesleyan University Press, 1957), 66. Barfield discusses how the development of human consciousness produced theories which assume that this consciousness does not exist. We describe phenomena as if our perceptions had no effect on them. "By treating the phenomena of nature as objects wholly extrinsic to man, with an origin and evolution of their own independent of man's evolution and origin, and then by endeavoring to deal with these objects as astronomy deals with celestial appearances . . . nineteenth-century science, and speculation succeeded in imprinting on the minds and imaginations of men their picture of an evolution of idols. One result of this has been to distort very violently our conception of the evolution of human consciousness. Or rather it has caused us to virtually deny such an evolution in the face of what must otherwise have been accepted as unmistakable evidence. . . . The biological picture of evolution was imprinted, it was the given framework into which they had to fit any theory they chose to form. Consequently in their endeavors to explain the mind of early men they set him down in fancy in front of phenomena identical with their own, but with his mind *tabla rasa*, and the supposed origin of human consciousness to lie in his first efforts to speculate about those phenomena," 124.

[30]Antonio Benítez Rojo, *The Repeating Island* (Durham: Duke University Press, 1992), 156, writes, "If we examine Lyotard's definition of postmodernity, it springs from a resistance to accepting the legitimacy of the discourses of the disciplines, since their presumed legitimacy rests upon their arbitrary appropriations as centers or genealogical origins, of one or the others past great fables or narratives. Post-modern literary analysis has at its heart the unmasking of the binary opposition." Further on he writes, "This difference, I repeat, is of the greatest importance, since other texts show the seams of their own arbitrariness . . . they ignore the huge and necessarily promiscuous archive that has been manipulated and severely edited by the authors of the narratives that they have chosen to be their foundational texts. Furthermore they construct themselves as astutely within an authentic fable of legitimation which inserts them directly into the discourse of power."

[31]This is an unexplored example of Mary Louise Pratt's concept of *anti-conquest*: the assertion of neutrality while at the same time power relations are being employed.

[32]According to Michael Holquist, in *The Dialogic Imagination*, heteroglossia is "the base condition governing the operation of meaning in any utterance, that which insures the primacy of context over text. At any given time, in any given place, there will be a set of conditions—social, historical, meteorological, physiological—that will insure that a word uttered in that place and at that time will have a meaning different than it would have under any other conditions," 428.

[33] Michael Wyatt, "Experience and Community: The Impact of 12 Step Program Theory on Theological Method," Ph.D. diss., Emory University, 1996.

[34] J.B. Pontalis, *Perdre de Vue* (Paris: Editions Gallimard, 1988), 289.

[35] Maurice Blanchot, "The Limits of Experience: Nihilism," in David B. Allison, ed., *The New Nietzsche* (Cambridge, Mass: MIT Press, 1985), 125-28.

[36] Antonio Gramsci, *Modern Prince* (New York: International Publishers, 1957), 58-59.

[37] Paolo Freire, *Pedagogy of Hope* (New York: Continuum Press, 1994), 85.

[38] Sergei Bocharov, "Conversations with Bakhtin," abridged from "About One Conversation and Its Context," *New Literary Review*, 2, 1993: 70-89. Trans. and ed. Vadim Liapunov.

[39] She continues, "Quite simply then critique is a mode of knowing that inquires into what is not said, into the silences and the suppressed or missing, in order to uncover the concealed operations of power and underlying socioeconomic relations connecting the myriad details and seemingly disparate events and representations of our lives. It shows how seemingly disconnected zones of culture are in fact linked through the highly differentiated and dispersed operation of a systematic logic of exploitation informing (affecting) all practices of society. . . . In sum then, critique disrupts that which represents itself as what is, as natural, as inevitable . . . and exposes 'what is' as socially and historically produced out of social contradictions which support inequality. It helps us explain how gender, race, class, and sexual oppression operate so we can change it," Teresa L. Ebert, *Cultural Critique*, Winter 1992: 9.

[40] I want to reiterate here that the manuscripts of Sommer, Spivak and Stoll have disturbed me deeply every time I have read them because of their assumptions and conclusions. The opinion stated here is cause for reflection on how scholars who lean toward the welfare of others, reconstructed Marxists included, become part of the non-dialogic practice of Western academic discourse. Little would be gained by focusing on the evil of incorrigible people so that we can feel better about ourselves.

[41] John Beverley, *Against Literature* (Minneapolis, University of Minnesota press, 1993), 35.

[42] Doris Sommer, "No Secrets: Rigoberta's Guarded Truth," *Womens Studies*, 1991, 20: 51-72.

[43] In *Beloved*, one of the driving images of Sethe's life is the rape of her milk by the white boys. Sommer writes that Menchú is being "coy"; that there is a possibility of "fictional seduction"; that "we would inevitably force her secrets into our framework" (Sommer 1991: 53). Thereafter she writes that Menchú is "[P]erforming a kind of rhetorical fictional seduction in which she lets the fringe of a hidden text show" (Sommer 1991: 54). She refers to

"[h]er [Menchú's] refusal of absolute intimacy," (Sommer 1991: 56). Further on, Sommer writes that Menchú "is performing a defensive move in the midst of her seduction" (Sommer 1991: 58). She refers to "[Menchú's] textual seduction" (Sommer 1991: 59).

[44]See Ujpan Bizaro, *Ignacio: The Diary of a Maya Indian of Guatemala*. Trans. Ignacio James Sexton (Pittsburgh: University of Pennsylvania Press, 1992), 97.

[45]Trinh Minh Ha, *When the Moon Waxes Red: Representation, Gender and Cultural Politics* (New York and London: Routledge, 1991), 68.

[46]Gayatri Chakavorty Spivak, "Can the Subaltern Speak?" in *Marxism and the Interpretation of Cultures* (Urbana: University of Illinois Press, 1988), 294.

[47]Antonio Gramsci, *Selections from the Political Writings 1910-1920* (London: Q. Hoare, Lawrence and Wishart, 1977), 12.

[48]David Stoll, *Between Two Armies in the Ixil Towns of Guatemala* (New York: Columbia University Press, 1993), 306.

[49]Conversation with Víctor Montejo, January 1995.

[50]The *Ladino* community members are not the only problem any more than the Korean shop keepers were the cause of the riots in Los Angeles in the Rodney King incident. But they were there, and there were sets of feelings about them and their relation to perceived power and access to justice and money.

[51]As we can see by reading Exodus, a pivotal text for Menchú, the Israelites, after their flight, complained that they wished that they never had left Egypt. In 1776, how many favored revolution? It is canonized because it was a success. In Freire we can see how those who have been made free through revolutionary process cannot maximize their freedom because they have no model for themselves. Freedom requires consciousness. Contemporary revolutions are seldom a complete success but rather a process of grating away at a power structure which wishes to suppress it.

I could argue that Mayans draw freely from the things that have influenced them, especially when those things are perceived as powerful. Why not use *Ladinos* as leaders? They are more accustomed to individual process.

[52]Rigoberta Menchú, *El Clamor de la Tierra*, 1993: 112-13.

[53]This inconsistency in her accounts are also mentioned by Víctor Perera in the bibliography of his book *Unfinished Conquest*. He mentions Payera's 1987 testimony of the Chajul massacre as deviating from that of Menchú. Her account has been questioned also by Marc Zimmermann, 1991.

[54]This process has been covered in theological tracts as well as in Foucault's essay on the idea of the shepherd.

[55]Churches seem to erupt in the backyards of families, gather congregations and splinter. They resemble the small congregations of Afro-American churches in the USA far more than the Southern Baptist Convention.

[56]Jean Molesky Poz, University of California at Berkeley, Native American Studies, is writing and translating narrative testimony on Mayan spirituality from day keepers in the area around Zunil. See also, Ricardo E. Lima Soto, *Aproximación a la Cosmovisión Maya*, 1995; *El Tzolkin, es más que un calendario*, CEDIM, 1995; and Daniel Matul, *Somos Un Solo Corazón* (Costa Rica: Liga Maya Internacional, 1994). See also, Víctor Perera, *Unfinished Conquest*.

[57]Víctor Montejo, *Testimony: Death of a Guatemalan Village*, trans. Víctor Perera (Willimantic, Conn.: Curbstone Press, 1987), 35.

[58]Víctor Montejo, "Oral tradition, an anthropological study of a Jacaltec Folktale," 1989, State University of New York at Albany.

[59]M.M. Bakhtin, *Toward a Philosophy of the Act*, 77-80. See also, Caryl Emerson, "Solov'ev, the Late Tolstoi and the Early M.M. Bakhtin on the Problem of Shame and Love," *Slavic Review*, 50, no. 3 (Fall 1991), 664.

[60]In M.M. Bakhtin, "all utterances are mediated because they can be viewed from the outside and interpreted by others." In this case, I refer to only the ability to speak.

[61]If we return to the *Philosophy of the Act*, we can see that M.M. Bakhtin perceives two options in verbal/personal response to a verbal interaction or text: 1) correctness or error, a grammatical non-interpretive investigation; 2) a 'creative' response (not to be confused with what in other writing is referred to as *creative understanding*) wherein the words are made to be whatever the interpreting group wishes. Both these options preclude the development of dialogue, because the speaker and his word fuse together. They do not necessarily conflate; one can appropriate the other. Fusing eliminates the possibility of growth, understanding or generation of a dialogical position, the third option.

[62]Caryl Emerson. "Solov'ev, the Late Tolstoi and the Early M.M. Bakhtin on the Problem of Shame and Love," *Slavic Review* 50, no. 3 (Fall 1991), 664.

[63]Rape also is mentioned on pp. 136-37, 142-43, 148, 173, 189, 198, and 235.

[64]Víctor Montejo, Conversations with Steve Kemper, undated article sent by author.

[65]Víctor Montejo, "El Kanil: Man of Lightning, trans. Wallace Kauffman (Carrboro: Signal Books, 1982), preface.

[66]In *Liberation of Theology*, Segundo argues for "the economy of energy in the process of love, which implies that there is some mechanism whereby we can

keep a whole host of people at arm's length so that we can effectively love a certain group of people. This mechanism is not precisely hatred, it is violence—at least some initial degree of violence. Segundo writes that the opposite of love is self-love—what M.M. Bakhtin calls *non-consummated actions* or *solipsism*. See also, John Pottinger, *The Political Theory of Liberation Theology* (NY: State University of New York Press, 1989), 60-85.

[67]Any assessment of death for political reasons (Vicente Menchú, for example) needs to consider this idea. See *Mea Cuba* of Gillermo Cabrera Infante 'Felos de se' (NY: Ferrar Straus Giroux, 1994). Cabrera Infante is a self-defined reactionary leftist whose family was devoutly Communist. He states: "Schopenhauer ends his disquisition with a note at once physical and spiritual: 'What makes suicide easier is that the physical pain associated with it loses all meaning in the eyes of someone affected by an excessive spiritual suffering. Such suffering applied to politics and combined with the idea of nation is, of course, patriotism. The last refuge of the scoundrel is converted thus into the nearest exit from historical life. . . . Generally one finds that when the terrors of life surpass the terror of death man puts an end to his days.' Durkheim, [he writes] classifies suicides into two groups: egoists and those with anomie, the first characteristic of our society, while the altruistic suicide (to the surprise of Marxists) is characteristic of primitive societies. . . . Inadmissible for religious and materialists alike, suicide ceases to be an undefinable problem when it is observed as an absolute ideology to be in the historical domain."

[68]Gary Saul Morson and Caryl Emerson, eds., *Rethinking Bakhtin*, 105-14.

[69]Fractals are produced by a set of equations that fluctuate between negative and positive infinity with the most turbulent section being the area from -1 to +1. They are self-referential and self-similar so that each *point of view* is composed of similar smaller points. The result of this is that absolute scale becomes meaningless. Whether the magnification of an image is one-to-one or one-to-one million, the pattern is the same. This lack of scale means that we can never know where we are simply by looking at the image. No matter how deeply one enters an image the sensation will remain that one is occupying the same space.

Bibliography

Alvarado, Walburga Rupflin. *El Tzolkin, es más que un calendario*. Ciudad de Guatemala: CEDIM, 1995.

Bakhtin, M.M. *Speech Genres and other Late essays*. Trans. Vern McGee. Austin: University of Texas Press, 1986.

____.Toward a Philosophy of the Act. Trans. Vadim Liapunov. University of Texas Press, 1993.

____. *Art and Answerability*. Trans. Michael Holquist and Vadim Liapunov. University of Texas Press, 1990.

____. *The Dialogic Imagination*. Trans. Michael Holquist and Caryl Emerson. University of Texas Press, 1981.

Barfield, Owen. *Saving the Appearances, a Study in Idolatry*. Middletown, Connecticut: Wesleyan University Press, 1957.

Benítez Rojo, Antonio. *The Repeating Island*. Durham: Duke University Press, 1992.

Beverley, John. *Against Literature*. Minneapolis: University of Minnesota Press, 1993.

____ and Marc Zimmermann. *Literature and Politics in the Central American Revolution*. University of Texas Press 1990.

Bizaro, Ujpan. *Ignacio: The Diary of a Maya Indian of Guatemala*. Trans. Ignacio James Sexton. Pittsburgh: University of Pennsylvania Press, 1992.

Cabrera, Edgar. *The Cosmogonía Maya*. San José, Costa Rica: Liga Maya Internacional, 1995.

Chiquito, Carlos Enrique. "Fundamentos históricos de la educación Maya." Ponencia presentada en el Primer Congreso de Educación Maya, Centro de estudios de la cultura Maya. Xelju', Guatemala, 9 de agosto 1994.

Chopp, Rebecca. *The Praxis of Suffering*. Maryknoll, New York: Orbis Books, 1986.

Cojti Cuxil, Demetrio. *Configuración del pensamiento político del Pueblo Maya*. Quetzaltenango, Guatemala: Asociación de escritores Mayences de Guatemala, 1991.

____. *Políticas para la reivindicación de los Mayas de hoy*. Ciudad de Guatemala: Seminario Permanente de Estudios Mayas, 1994.

Colop, Enrique Sam. "Maya Poetics." Ph.D. diss., State University of New York, December 1994.

Deane, Seamus. *Nationalism, Colonialism and Literature*. University of Minnesota Press, 1990.

DeCerteau, Michel. *Heterologies, Discourse on the Other.* University of Minnesota Press, 1986.

Enríquez Cojulun, Berta Cleotilde. "Zunil y su mundo precolombino." Ph.D. diss., Universidad de San Carlos de Guatemala, Quetzaltenango, 1968.

Estrada Monroy, Agustín. "Vida esotérica Maya-K'ekchi." *Edición Cultura.* Ciudad de Guatemala: Ministerio de Cultura y Deportes, 1990.

Foucault, Michael. *The Archeology of Knowledge.* New York: Pantheon, 1972.

Freire, Paulo. *Pedagogy of the Oppressed.* New York: Continuum Publishing Co., 1985.

_____. *Pedagogy of Hope.* New York: Continuum Publishing Co., 1994.

González Gaspar, Pedro. *A Mayan Life.* Rancho Palos Verdes, California: Yax Te' Press, 1995.

Gramsci, Antonio. *Selections from the Prison Writings.* London: Q. Hoare, Lawrence and Wishart, 1977.

_____. *The Modern Prince.* New York: International Publishers, 1957.

Gutiérrez, Gustavo. *The Theology of Liberation.* Orbis Books, 1988.

Hulme, Peter. *Colonial Encounters.* London: Chapman & Hall, 1987.

Instituto Centroamericano de Estudios Políticos, eds. *Identidad y derechos de los pueblos indígenas.* Ciudad de Guatemala: INCEP, 1993.

Kuhn, Thomas. *The Structure of Scientific Revolutions.* Chicago: University of Chicago Press, 1970.

Menchú, Rigoberta y Comité de Unidad Campesina. *El clamor de la tierra.* Donostia: Hirugarén Prensa, 1992.

Montejo, Víctor. *El Kanil Man of Lightning,* Trans. Wallace Kauffman. Carrboro, North Carolina: Signal Press, 1982.

_____. "Oral Tradition: an anthropological study of a Jacaltec Folktale." Master's thesis, State University of New York at Albany, 1989.

_____. *Testimony: Death of a Guatemalan Village.* Trans. Víctor Perera. Willamic, Conn.: Curbstone Press, 1987.

_____. *The Bird who Cleans the World.* Trans. Víctor Perera and Wallace Kauffman. Curbstone Press, 1991.

_____. "The Dynamics of Cultural Resistance and Transformations: The Case of Guatemalan Mayan Refugees in Mexico." Ph.D. diss., University of Connecticut, 1993.

_____ and Q'Anil Akab. *Brevísima relación testimonial de la continua destrucción del Mayab'.* Providence, Rhode Island: Guatemalan Scholars Network, 1992.

Morson, Gary Saul and Caryl Emerson. *Rethinking Bakhtin*. Evanston: Northwestern University Press, 1989.

Perera, Víctor. *Unfinished Conquest*. Berkeley: University of California Press, 1993.

Pontlis, J.B. *Perdre de vue*. Paris: Editions Gallimard, 1988.

Pottinger, John. *The Political Theory of Liberation Theology*. New York: State University of New York Press, 1989.

Pratt, Mary Louise. *Imperial Eyes*. London: Routledge, 1992.

Rojas Lima, Flavio. *La Cofradía: Reducto Cultural Indígena*. Ciudad de Guatemala: Litografías Modernas, 1988.

Román-Lagunas, Jorge, ed. *La literatura Centroamericana, visiones y revisiones*. Lewiston: The Edwin Mellen Press, 1994.

Ricoeur, Paul. *Soi meme comme un autre* (One's Self as Another). Trans. Kathleen Blamey. Chicago: University of Chicago Press, 1992.

Rivera, Roberto. "The Oppositional Nature of Liberation Discourse." (publication pending, 1995).

Segundo, Juan. *The Liberation of Theology*. Orbis Books, 1976.

Smith, Carol. *Guatemalan Indians and the State*. University of Texas Press, 1992.

Solares, Jorge. *Estado y nación: las demandas de los grupos étnicos en Guatemala*. Identidad y Derechos de los Pueblos Indígenas. Ciudad de Guatemala: INCEP (Instituto Centroamericana de Estudios Políticos), 1993.

Somos Matul, Daniel. *Un Solo Corazón*. Costa Rica: Liga Maya Internacional, 1994.

Spivak, Gayatri Chakavorty. "Can the Subaltern speak?" *Marxism and the Interpretation of Culture*. Urbana: University of Illinois Press, 1988.

Stoll, David. *Between Two Armies in the Ixil Towns of Guatemala*. New York: Columbia University Press, 1993.

_____ and Virginia Garrad-Burnett. *Rethinking Protestantism in Latin America*. Philadelphia: Temple University Press, 1993.

Trinh, Minh Ha. *When the Moon Waxes Red: Representation, Gender and Cultural Politics*. Routledge, 1991.

Vgotsky, Lev. *Thought and Language*. Boston: MIT University Press, 1962.

Warren, Kay B. *The Symbolism of Subordination, Indian Identity in a Guatemalan Town*. University of Texas Press, 1989.

Yudice, George and Jean Franco. *On Edge, The Crisis of Contemporary Latin American Culture*. University of Minnesota Press, 1989.

Zimmermann, Marc and John Beverley. *Literature and Politics in the Central American Revolutions.* University of Texas Press, 1990.

Periodicals and Articles

Amar Sánchez, Ana María. "La ficción del testimonio." *Revista Iberoamericana* (April 1990): 447.

Aton, Adrianne. "*Testimonio*: a Bridge between Psychotherapy and Sociotherapy." *Women and Therapy* 13 (1992): 173.

Barnet, Miguel. "La novela testimonio y socio-literatura." *La Fuente Viva.* Habana: Editorial Letras Cubanas, 1983.

Beverely, John. "Through All Things Modern: Second Thoughts on the Testimonial." *Boundary* 2, v. 18 (Summer 1991): 1.

Blanchot, Maurice. "The Limits of Experience: Nihilism." *The New Nietzche.* MIT Press, 1985.

Brittin, Alice, 1993. "Close Encounters of the Third World Kind: Rigoberta Menchú's and Elizabeth Burgos' *Me llamo Rigoberta Menchú*." Unpublished manuscript.

Bocharov, Sergey. "About One Conversation and Its Context from *Conversations with Bakhtin*." *New Literary Review* (Moscow) 2 (1993): 70-89. Trans. Vadim Liapunov.

Cojti Cuxil, Demetrio. "Universidades guatemaltecas, universidades colonialistas." Unpublished draft.

"Expectaciones del Pueblo Maya, hacia una organización política." Ciudad de Guatemala, 22 de noviembre de 1991.

Feal, Rosemary. "Spanish American Ethnobiography and the Slave Narrative Tradition." *Modern Language Studies* (Winter 1990).

Foster, David William. "Latin American Documentary Narrative." *PMLA* 99, no. 1 (January 1984).

Jara, René and Vidal Hernán. "Testimonio y Literatura." Minneapolis: Institute for the Study of Ideologies and Literature, Society for the Study of Contemporary Hispanic and Lusophone Revolutionary Literatures, 1986: entire volume.

López Raquec, Margarita. "Implicaciones de la atomización lingüística en el idioma Kachikel." Paper presented at the American Anthropological Association, Chicago, 1991.

Martínez-Echazabal, Lourdes. "Translating Latin America, Culture as Text." State University of New York at Binghamton, 1991.

Menchú, Rigoberta. "The Indigenous Future." *Christianity and Crisis* 53 (1 February 1993): 19.

Menchú, Rigoberta. "The Mayan Way." *New Perspectives Quarterly* 11 (Summer 1994).

Montejo, Víctor. "In the name of the pot the sun the broken speak the Rock the stick the idol ad infinitum and ad nauseam: an expose of anglo anthropologists obsessions with and invention of mayan gods." Paper presented at the American Anthropological Association, November 1991.

Pop Caal, Antonio. "Raíces históricas de la colonización cristiana." Unpublished manuscript, October 1991.

Otzoy, Irma. "Mayan Clothing and Identity." Paper presented at the American Anthropological Association, November 1991.

_____ and Enrique Sam Colop. "Mayan Ethnicity and Modernization." Paper presented at the American Anthropological Association, 1988.

Pansini, Jude. "Ethnic Identity in Guatemala." Unpublished draft.

Salazar, Claudia. "Rigoberta's Narrative and the New Practice of Oral History." *Women and Language* 13, no. 1: 8.

Riccio Allesandra. "Lo testimonial y la novela testimonial." *Revista Iberoamericana* 56 (1990).

Said, Edward. "Permission to Narrate" *The London Review of Books* (16 February 1992).

Sklodowska, Elizbeta. "Testimonio mediatiado: ventriloquia o heteroglosia." *Revista de Crítica Literaria Latinoamericana* 19, no. 38 (Lima 1993).

_____. "Hacia una bibliografía sobre el testimonio hispanoamericano." *Chasqui: Revista de Literatura Latinoamericana* 1 (Provo, Utah, 20 May 1991).

_____. "Miguel Barnet: Hacia la poética de la novela testimonial." *Revista de Crítica Literaria Latinoamericana* 27, no. 1 (Lima, 1988).

Sommer, Doris. "No Secrets, Rigoberta's Guarded Truth." *Women's Studies* 20 (1991): 51-72.

Walker, Anne and Ricardo Suárez. "Asserting Our Dignity." *The Harvard International Review* 17, no. 1 (Winter 1995).

Warren, Kay B. "Four Fallacies on Indianness in Latin America." Paper presented at the American Anthropological Association, Phoenix, 1988.

Yudice, George. "*Testimonio* and Postmodernism: Who does Testimonial Writing Represent?" *Latin American Perspectives* 18 (Summer 1991): 15-18.

Zimmermann, Marc. "El otro de Rigoberta: los testimonias de Ignacio Bizaro Ujpan y la resistencia en Guatemala." *Revista Crítica Literaria Latin Americana* 18 (Lima, 1992): 229-43.

_____ and Raul Rojas, eds. "Guatemala: voces desde el silencio." *Abrazo* (March 1993).

Video and Film

Menchú, Rigoberta. *Broken Silence*. Princeton: Films for the Humanities and Sciences, 1993.

Amlin, Patricia. *Popul-Vuh: Creation Story of the Maya Quiché*. San Francisco State University: Feature length animated film (English, Spanish, Quiché). Address: SFU, 19th Avenue and Holloway, San Francisco, CA 94132.

Information on Guatemalan/Mayan Affairs

CEDIM: Centro de Documentación e Investigación Maya.
11 Calle Nueve 44
Zona 1, No. 5
Guatemala City, Guatemala

Colas, Santiago
Assistant Professor, Latin American and Comparative Literature
University of Michigan
Ann Arbor, MI 48109-1275

The Guatemalan Scholars Network
c/o Marilyn Moors
1014 Buffalo Run Road
Friedsville, Maryland 21531

INCEP: Instituto Centroamericano de Estudios Políticos
12 Calle 6-40
Zona 9, Oficina 301-2
Guatemala City, Guatemala

La Lengua Maya Internacional
Apto. 584 Código 1100
San Juan de Tibas, Costa Rica

The Latin American Studies Assn.
946 Pitt Union
University of Pittsburgh
Pittsburgh, PA 15260
Internet: LASA+@PITT.EDU

Washington Office on Latin America
400 C Street NE
Washington, DC 20002